IN CASE
OF ANY
NEWS

IN CASE OF
ANY NEWS

A Diary of Living and Dying

KENNETH ROY

Foreword by
SALLY MAGNUSSON

Introduction by
MAGNUS LINKLATER

I C S *Books*

BY THE SAME AUTHOR

Travels in a Small Country
Conversations in a Small Country
The Closing Headlines
Alastair Hetherington: A Man of His Word (Editor)
Both Sides of the Border
The Invisible Spirit: A Life of Post-War Scotland 1945–1975
The Broken Journey: A Life of Scotland 1976–1999

ACKNOWLEDGEMENTS

The publishers wish to express their appreciation to Sally Magnusson, Magnus Linklater and Ian Jack, and to Tom Johnstone and James Hutcheson of Birlinn for their practical assistance in bringing this book to press.

First published in the United Kingdom in 2019 by
ICS Books
216 Liberator House
Prestwick Airport
Prestwick KA9 2PT

Copyright 2019 Kenneth Roy

Printed in the United Kingdom by Bell & Bain Ltd., Glasgow.

British Library Cataloguing-in-Publication Data
A catalogue record for this book is available from the British Library

ISBN 978-0-9546527-9-1

To the magnificent team in Station 9,
University Hospital Ayr,
with overwhelming gratitude and affection

CONTENTS

FOREWORD

Sally Magnusson

What hard and lonely work dying can be.

I was reading this book as a dear relative laboured towards her end. At 93 her infirmities made living less appealing than it was for 73-year-old Kenneth Roy, who had so much still to do and say. But at her bedside I realised that Kenneth had expressed what dying was like for her too: the bewildering unreality of knowing that death is approaching and nothing now can stop it; the awful fear of this being the night you won't wake in the morning; the mounting physical indignities so difficult to tolerate with grace.

Kenneth's most overwhelming discovery in his final weeks was also one I was seeing before my eyes: the warm and cheerful care of NHS staff (and in our case the local council's homecare angels), who made lingering dying as near to comfortable as it gets.

Searingly personal as Kenneth's narrative is, in those ways it speaks to and for us all. It reminds us what we have in our National Health Service. It articulates truths and joys and horrors about the human condition itself.

Kenneth does it by reaching one last time for the precious commodity that had always been his trade. This is a man who loved words, recognised their potency, respected their meaning and demanded rigour in our dealings with them. Only three paragraphs into the first day of his hospital diary he can't resist drawing attention to a subbing error in *The Times*:

'Close to the end, however... I consider myself liberated from all grammatical preferences, mine or anybody else's, and from any general obligation to write "well". Bugger style. All I have left is substance, and maybe not much of that.

'Close to the end, which was where I started this thought, as I start most thoughts these days, I am still capable of being irked by subbing errors.'

And there you have the flavour of this extraordinary diary, and of the man himself in all his blithe contrariness – here announcing himself free from any constraints of grammatical style, life being, well, so short, but on the other hand not yet too short to be miffed by someone else's solecisms.

A wayward stream of consciousness like this might sound the alarm in the hands of a lesser wordsmith, but here it becomes the perfect vehicle for the observations that Kenneth taps out each day, typing, typing for dear life. The style is conversational, pacey, syntactically immaculate (whatever he might say) and at times quite agonisingly intimate. It is not, as Kenneth doubtless knew fine, the slightest bit buggered.

The publishers have respected Kenneth's hope that his work be reproduced as he wrote it, just short of the 50,000 words he was aiming for. 'The thing must stand on its own, forever imperfect,' he writes, 'dashed off like an overnight review from the Glasgow Pavilion when the final curtain hasn't quite fallen.' At least it's good to know that his eternal rest will not be disturbed by any subbing concerns.

But what is this thing that stands before us on its own, full of good words that on occasion rise to beautiful flights of eloquence? It's a wry lament for life. A minute description of physical failure. A belated reckoning with aspects of his past. A passionate celebration of the love of professional strangers who, for a few momentous weeks in the autumn of 2018, became family.

And because Kenneth never lost his sense of humour, it's often bleakly, waspishly funny. On being given a short time to live, he 'did half-think of asking what my chances were of having to sit through another Hogmanay show.' Thinking about the difficult relationship with his father, he has 'arrived at the tentative conclusion that no good purpose would be served by a celestial reunion.'

Late one night he muses sadly on the utter incomprehensibility of his plight: 'This bed, is it really my death bed? That ticking clock with the wrong date, could it be the last thing I hear? Do I really leave the world facing two signs that say TOILET?'

We smile at that last sentence, because it's witty. Only, not for long, because we don't understand death either, and because a toilet sign is likely to be the last thing many of us do see, and because Kenneth will all too soon be proved right himself. And our throats constrict with the pity of it. It's the hospital staff who enable him to fulfil his determination to write this book, devoting themselves to his 'final act of creativity' in ways that touch Kenneth to

11

the core. Their skilled caring nourishes his spirit and the extra medical procedures, thoughtfully planned, deliver him enough time to sign off his life in the way he so deeply craves.

He knows the value of what these people, along with his faithful visitors, are giving him, and we look on in a kind of awe as this proud, clever man absorbs the very last lesson of his life:

'Overwhelming love. Overwhelming love. Overwhelming love. I am surrounded by it, wrapped in it, and I am trying at the end of my life to learn how to deal with it.'

INTRODUCTION

Magnus Linklater

_____

I always thought of Kenneth Roy as the conscience of Scotland – a writer who gave the nation a wee nudge when he thought it had strayed off course. Or a sharp crack on the shin when it had got something seriously wrong. He always believed that journalism should keep a watching brief on the vagaries of society, and in the *Scottish Review*, which he edited and to which he contributed for 23 years, he gave space to investigations of injustice, overweening bureaucracy, and those in high places who had betrayed their trust. These things made him angry, and he never wrote better than when he was in a state of simmering outrage.

If this suggests a dour or embittered approach, it is wide of the mark. Kenneth relished the absurdity of life, and enjoyed celebrating its lighter side. He was above all an observer, recording the eccentricities of his fellow human beings, and digging into forgotten corners of his country's history. He warmed to those who had fallen by the wayside of life, rather than those who had risen to high places, which made his role as founder and publisher of *Who's Who in Scotland* – an indispensable guide to the high heid yins of the Scottish establishment – something of an irony, as he himself was wont to point out.

Above all, he loved writing, and he would give space in his magazine to any article that was well crafted, whether or not it had contemporary relevance. His own account of 'The Road to Inveramsay' (*Scottish Review*, Summer 2001) is a wonderful exercise in literary ability, as well as a powerful reflection on the vanished past of the Scotland he loved. He had made it his business to track down a long disused station on the Aberdeen line, where once a railway clerk and a shunter met every evening to talk about life, the world and 'everything in heaven and earth'; they called it Utopia. Kenneth used that story to write an essay about the loss of an intellectual tradition that he valued and which he emulated himself. It brings a tear to the eye, and it is beautifully written. As the journalist Ian Jack observed, in a tribute at Kenneth's memorial, 'his prose was clear, vivid and direct, and often tinged with irony and anger; and with cantankerousness – we shouldn't forget that; but most memorably of all with humour'.

No wonder, then, that Kenneth should have recorded his own last illness in the same wry style, and that he should spend his final weeks in hospital writing to the very end. Not just writing, but completing a proper book, all 49,000 words of it, which is now published here. Announcing his impending death in the *Review*, he had written that he was 'on the last bus now, front row nearest the driver, and heading for the terminus. And hoping all the traffic lights are at red.'

Sadly, they remained relentlessly at green, and Kenneth had only a few weeks more to live. But how he used that late stoppage time – as he, the football fan, might have described it.

He regrets, but does not bemoan, being taken so early. 'I've never thought of 73 as an age to die,' he writes. 'It's a score in the Open Championship, respectable enough but on the fringes of contention at best, unless the wind blows, when 73 on a links can feel like 65.' One of his journalistic heroes, Bill Deedes, late of the *Daily Telegraph*, had carried on until his mid-90s, dying in mid-sentence as he tapped out his last column on an ancient Remington typewriter. 'I used to complain that Deedes should have done the decent thing and finished the piece. That joke, like so many, is dust in the mouth. I shall not after all live to the grand old age of a Deedes, but be taken at 73 by the random banality of cancer.'

Both he, and Dr Gillen, his consultant, realise that the book he has embarked on is prolonging his life. What begins as a diary of his last days, becomes instead an exploration of the themes of life and death. He goes back to his childhood, his unhappy schooldays, the friendships he formed, and the people who mattered to him, recalling small and large events in a life which, as he taps away at his laptop, becomes more dramatic than perhaps he imagined, including a close brush with death in a crashed plane. He explores his own faith, or lack of it, remembering philosophers like Seneca, or the few church ministers who influenced him, and whose sermons he enjoyed. In the end, however, he finds himself agreeing with David Hume, who, interviewed on his deathbed by James Boswell (Kenneth admires the scoop) rejected outright the idea of immortality. 'I am with David Hume,' he writes. 'It is the only theory that makes any sense. Very soon now, I am heading for extinction as certainly as David Hume 242 years ago; and resigned to it. Like him, I dislike ignorant crowds, whether of body or spirit makes no difference. I'll take annihilation any time. And there's an end of it.'

It is clear that the team of nurses who care for him (and to whom he dedicates the book) see him as more than just an ordinary patient. They confide in him, and he in them. A nurse, supervising one of his intimate moments, remarks: 'Kenneth, you are peeing for Scotland.' He responds: 'Then it is my only representative honour, even if it has come comparatively late in life.' Audrey, a member of staff on the ward, offers to order a new mattress 'in case my bum develops bedsores; apparently it's already a bit red. I accept. As far as I'm concerned, Audrey's word is gospel. She already knows more about my rear end than any woman has a right to know.'

He brings out the best in them, and they become part of the cast list of his dying days, as do his family, and his faithful colleagues and friends – Fiona MacDonald, Islay McLeod and Barbara Millar, who bring him dry sherry, Saint Agur cheese and watermelon, the final pleasures he is able to enjoy.

Writing to the end, he realises that he is surrounded by 'overwhelming love ... I am trying at the end of my life to learn how to deal with it and respond to it. It isn't easy. It's the most difficult thing I've ever done.'

When, finally, he decides that the time has come to let go, he signs off with only one small regret – that he did not reach 50,000 words. 'I've finished 1,000 words light,' he writes. 'Shame, but too bad.'

There is not much to add to what Kenneth himself recalls of his own life, but inevitably, since he turns self-deprecation into an art-form, he plays down his journalistic achievements, and is sparing on the biographical detail. He and his sister Linda were brought up in Bonnybridge, near Falkirk, where their father and mother were involved in amateur theatre. Kenneth went to Denny High School, which he left 'as soon as legally possible', and began work as a junior reporter on the *Falkirk Mail*, receiving expenses instead of a salary. He had been the paper's Bonnybridge correspondent since the age of 13, being paid, as he enjoys recalling, in postage stamps. When the title folded, he joined the *Falkirk Herald*, then later the *Greenock Evening Telegraph*. By the mid-1960s he was working for the *Glasgow Herald*, where his colleague, Ian Jack, recalled a story they did together on the Blackhill housing scheme, which was then notorious as a rough area of the city.

'In those days, the *Glasgow Herald* didn't do that kind of social inquiry,' said Jack. 'It held aloof among the fur coats of Buchanan Street, far from the mire of crime and personal tragedy that was ploughed by the *Express* and the *Record*. So it felt enterprising for us to take a cab to Blackhill and pull out our notebooks and ask people what it was like to live there. Kenneth wrote the piece, contrary to a later memory of his that I had written it, and as I remember it was judicious and sympathetic about a place that was frightening and terrible but nevertheless filled with people no less human than we were.'

In June 1967 he married Margaret, who survives him with their sons Stephen and Christopher. The family began life in a Victorian villa in Kirknewton, south of Edinburgh, and after a number of moves ended up in Ayrshire, close to his office overlooking Prestwick Airport. From there, in later years, he wrote *The Invisible Spirit* and *The Broken Journey*, both about modern Scotland – about the resilience of its people, and the systems that had failed them.

When he left the *Herald*, Alastair Warren, the editor, predicted that he 'could have had a promising future in journalism'; instead, he went briefly into public relations, before embarking on a series of publishing ventures, some more successful than others. Even those that fell by the wayside were, in their time, memorable. *Scottish Theatre*, a monthly magazine, contributed a commentary – today sadly lacking – on the state of drama in Scotland, before running into financial difficulties. He himself wrote two plays, one of which at least was headed for the stage, with the actor Bill Paterson in a lead role. But the National Theatre of Scotland prevaricated, and finally failed to respond – the memory of it still caused Kenneth a surge of resentment. *The Journalist's Handbook* was, for a decade, an essential guide to the newspaper and media world, with contributions from distinguished names north and south of the border, though the best and most acerbic critiques came from Kenneth's own pen. *Who's Who in Scotland*, founded in 1986, survives to this day, thicker each year as it become recognised as an essential guide, and less than a decade later, he started the *Scottish Review*.

By then he had worked for Radio Scotland, presented news and current affairs programmes for BBC television, and launched an independent radio franchise, before going back to newspapers and writing for the newly launched *Scotland on Sunday*, followed by *The Observer* and *The Scotsman*, winning columnist of the year at the 1994 UK Press Awards.

He preferred being his own master, however, and it was the *Scottish Review* which he moulded to his shape. It featured essays, biography, contemporary history, travel writing – anything that caught his attention. People wrote for it, not because of the fees – they were negligible – but because they recognised and appreciated an unbiased but committed forum for views about modern Scotland. When it went online, it was able to run long investigations, most of them Kenneth's own, into such things as the case of Annie Börjesson, the young Swedish woman whose body was found on a beach in Ayrshire in 2005, and whose death was a mystery until Kenneth unpicked it; or the suicides of the two teenage girls who plunged to their deaths from the Erskine Bridge in October 2009.

He loved Scotland, warts and all, but he did not hesitate to expose the warts. He could not bear the 'Here's to us, wha's like us?' mentality because of its smug self-satisfaction and intellectual laziness. He disliked nationalism – with a small n – although at the same time he argued that Scotland was being treated as an 'unthreatening backwater distinguished by the poor education, poor health and poor housing of its people'. What he distrusted was populism and the mob mentality. Whenever a trend in popular thinking emerged, his instinct almost always took him in the opposite direction.

He was pleased with the fact that no-one could attach a political label to him, and he never publicly backed any political party. Only on the day before the independence referendum in 2014 did he break his own rule with a blistering attack on the Yes campaign. But this was on the grounds of its divisive nature and the damage the referendum had done to his country.

He was a football fan, who liked to champion the lower league sides, like Mansfield Town, Oldham Athletic, Crewe Alexandra, Tranmere Rovers, whose names took him back to the age of footballers in long trousers and Brylcreemed hair. His own favourite in the Scottish league was East Stirlingshire whose downward spiral he notes with sympathy. He would listen to the football results coming in on a Saturday afternoon and could, if you were so interested, update you on a Monday morning.

He enjoyed the company of his fellow journalists, and the intimacy of those who worked with him. With them he could be relaxed and gregarious. Yet there was always something held back, a self-containment that made him more the onlooker than the participant. He was not the kind of reporter who lunched contacts or received tip-offs from insiders; he sniffed out most of his stories sitting at his computer. He had a nose for an exclusive, buried in the boring bits of official or annual reports. In this he was like Claud Cockburn, the legendary founder of *The Week* in the 1930s, who once, stuck in Spain and without a lead for the magazine, found a torn piece of newspaper in the gutter, and wrote an entire issue based on the headline.

When devolution came, Kenneth seized on it as an opportunity to give some intellectual shape to the new Scotland. He launched the Institute of Contemporary Scotland and invited members to join the debate. The intent was, in his own words, 'to recapture the rough democracy of Scotland and encourage the powerful and powerless to share the same space'. Whatever the reason, the Institute never lived up to its billing. What stemmed from it, however, was to become his greatest achievement – the Young Scotland Programme, which later became the

Young Programme charity spanning the UK and Ireland. He refers to it as his 'pride and joy', and that knocks on the head any idea that he was merely the cynical critic of his times. He believed profoundly in the potential of youth. The idea was, as Kenneth himself put it 'to encourage and engage a neglected group in our society – people who have left full-time education and are now building careers'. He drew on the story of Inveramsay and those who gathered in the railway shack called Utopia, to encourage young people to talk about themselves, their world, and the possibilities ahead. The debaters of Inveramsay 'inhabited a different world', he wrote, 'but their idealism and independent spirit go on inspiring our programme. We can all build a shack we call Utopia, if not on the station platform, then in our hearts and minds.'

He planned every last detail of the programmes and arranged for unusual speakers to come, mainly to describe their own, often challenging, experiences. He never interfered, but he did offer participants the chance to express themselves, and to be adventurous. It is no coincidence that the first Young Scotland Programme had a poster, which hangs in the office to this day, with the slogan 'Thinking for ourselves'. Blind acceptance was alien to him and he was frustrated when he saw it in others. He thought the young were the best route to challenging the status quo and he made them aware of their own potential. He had the ability to make anyone he was talking to feel as if they were the most interesting person in the room.

That, undoubtedly, was what lay behind the devotion of his hospital team, as he penned his final words. The book he leaves behind is remarkable, not just because it was written by a dying man; not just because it is finely crafted, full of wit and detailed recollection; but because it is a model of how to cope with impending death. It will stand as a testament to a life well led, and a death that is addressed honestly, unsparingly and with the utmost courage. Inevitably, Kenneth nominated himself as its reviewer:

'It is emotionally honest, I hope it's even funny in places, and it is publishable as it stands. It only lacks a conclusion, and I don't have one, I'm still working on it in my head. I have to be open to the possibility that I'll never get that far. I take no hour for granted.'

In Case of Any News

Thursday 4 October

IT IS OFFICIAL: I am dying of cancer. I know this because *The Times*, once known as the paper of record, carries a news story bylined Magnus Linklater and headed: '*Scottish Review* editor reveals terminal cancer'. I avoided using the word in the *SR* valedictory, no doubt because there may be a tiny furtive part of me that is still in denial. My father died of the same thing (lung in his case) at 63. I have managed an extra decade, but it's hardly an impressive record. Bang goes my hope of emulating the feat of Bill Deedes who expired over the Remington mid-sentence of his last column at 90-something. I used to complain that Deedes should have done the decent thing and finished the piece. That joke, like so many, is dust in the mouth. I shall not after all live to the grand old age of a Deedes, but be taken at 73 by the random banality of cancer.

Two of my friends, William Hunter and John Moorhouse, went at the same age. I remember thinking they'd rather let the side down. Hunter died alone in his wee bungalow in Newton Mearns, Moorhouse took ill while on holiday in Italy, far from his beloved Yorkshire. But I've never thought of 73 as an age to die. It's a score in the Open Championship, respectable enough but on the fringes of contention at best, unless the wind blows, when 73 on a links can feel like 65.

Today's *Times* also carries an only slightly abbreviated version of the *SR* editorial as its op-ed. A touching gesture for which I thank the Magnuses Llewellyn and Linklater. Close to the end, however, and for some reason I have always had an aversion to qualifying a sentiment with the word 'however', too stiff a usage, but I no longer care… I consider myself liberated from all grammatical preferences, mine or anybody else's, and from any general obligation to write 'well'. Bugger style. All I have left is substance, and maybe not much of that.

Close to the end, which was where I started this thought, as I start most thoughts these days, I am still capable of being irked by subbing errors. I'd quoted in my piece the final paragraph of *The Dead* – with its haunting incantation of the snow being 'general all over Ireland' – as one of my favourite passages in literature. But the snow this morning is no longer general. In *The Times* version it seems to be snowing 'generally', which suggests that it might be okay somewhere over on the far west.

It's almost 10.30pm. About 45 minutes ago, the tube in my nose (which extended all the way down to the stomach, aspirating old blood, of which there is rather a lot it seems) suddenly popped out and fell soundlessly to the floor. I called the duty nurse, young Christina from Stornoway, and explained the all too visible nature of the calamity, adding feebly that it was the first time this had happened since the tube and I made our acquaintance 36 hours ago. Christina thought perhaps it was her bad luck. She is so sweet. I uttered consoling words. But shamefully, I didn't own up to the probable reason for the technical malfunction, which had nothing to do with Hebridean superstition. Anyway, here I am waiting for a replacement so that I can spend a second night propped up on the pillows trying not to disturb the tube.

Just before the first tube and I parted company so unexpectedly, I'd been speaking on the phone to an important friend, very much in the news these days, who is in Nottingham for a hearing of some sort. She didn't sound too happy about being in Nottingham and had been looking forward to returning to London until she heard that the place where her committee was due to meet in Southwark had been flooded. She was now facing the possibility of having to continue meeting in Nottingham, of all places.

After our conversation, I had a keen longing to be in Nottingham myself, padding the streets of an English provincial city for copy, as I had once done every week for *The Observer*, propping up a bar in the evening before seeking out some half-decent Italian restaurant and going to bed with a few serviceable phrases for the week's instalment of 'Kenneth Roy's Britain' swimming in my head.

In fact I was now in danger of getting positively sentimental about Nottingham. Not that I've been, nor ever will be now – though I used to follow its football team when it was managed by that dodgy genius Clough – but rather Nottingham as a metaphor for the sunny upland, so casually assumed, of all that is past and never to be again. So I cried, silly sod, thinking about the sense of loss that Nottingham suddenly symbolised for me, and that's how the tube popped out. It couldn't cope with such a lachrymose exhibition and decided it would rather be on the floor than up my nose, and I really couldn't blame it.

When the replacement arrived, it was close to midnight. They tried three times, but I gagged each time and eventually it was agreed that I'd suffered enough for one night. I took a sleeping pill, which they give me every night, and buried myself in the high bed, shaking, until the tablet did the trick and I fell into a dreamless sleep.

Friday 5 October

NEXT WEEK will be my third in the hospital if I last here that long, because by then I'll have received such treatment as they are able to give me for the time being and I shall have to 'move on', as the dying do. A consultant in palliative care has just been to see me, wondering about my needs. It isn't long before we agree that what I need most is privacy, thus ruling out an obvious local facility where the frail elderly are accommodated in old-fashioned wards. I'd rather die.

Yesterday, John Mosey, whose 19-year-old daughter Helga, a promising musician, was killed in the Lockerbie air disaster, asked Fiona if she thought I was a believer, because according to John – a minister of the Congregational church in Lancashire – on the few occasions he'd met me, I had struck him as a spiritual person. John, in one of our conversations, spoke of his faith in what he calls 'the bigger picture': he is convinced that he will meet Helga again in the next life. I refrained from asking what form she might take. I'm genuinely curious.

I can't share his certainty, but I envy it. It must be the ultimate consolation. But perhaps not for everyone, as I'll illustrate by reference to my father Richard (Dick or Dickie as he was known in Bonnybridge).

First I have to ask myself whether such a meeting would fill either of us with joy. Dick – as my mother Esther called him – was not without talent, most of it dissipated in booze, Woodbines and self-pity. When his mother died in a flu epidemic, the one just after the first war, his father Fred despatched him to live with two bachelor brothers who kept a shop in the village, while Fred formed a new attachment with a nice woman called Mary and together they had a son, also called Fred – 'Young Fred' for the avoidance of doubt. Meanwhile, poor Dick continued to live above the shop, a boy who had lost his mother and been abandoned by his father. There was a reason for the self-pity; it cannot be denied. But daddy's way of coping was to drown in it. When he was not out 'seeing a man about a dog' – the man in question being available for consultation only during opening hours, while the mysterious dog never ventured far from its distant, possibly imaginary kennel – he was slumped on the sofa bemoaning his wretched lot and beseeching his only son to 'Be Somebody'. It was a command that I found intimidating. What was this 'Somebody' I was to be? What had a 10-year-old boy done to deserve such a burden of expectation?

I said he was not without talent. He was a director of plays, what they used to call in the amateur theatre a producer, and was skilful, even artistic, in moving and grouping characters. He built an elaborate cardboard stage and spent hours on Sunday afternoons – a rare interlude in the licensing week when there were no men to see about dogs – arranging his toy characters around it, in preparation for his next production in the Public Hall. His favourite play was the obscure *Six Characters in Search of an Author*, but reckoning that there was no market in Bonnybridge for Luigi Pirandello, he tended to play safe with the working-class dramas of the socialist miner Joe Corrie, a local favourite.

I will say more about my daddy if I get the time. Meanwhile I've arrived at the tentative conclusion that no good purpose would be served by a celestial reunion. But I must be open to the possibility that others, including perhaps Dick himself, will take a different view.

Now, a word about that chancer Seneca. Regret recommending him for my literary bucket list. Like a good Stoic, he embraces the imminence of death. Every time he sneezes he is begging for it: come, bring it on, see if he cares. Why fear death, he asks, when we have been dead before? We were dead before we were born. We shall be dead again, a second and final time. This is known as Seneca's two deaths theory. It has survived as a respectable idea for more than two thousand years. I wonder why.

Consider the logic in my own case. Yes, it is true that I was non-existent before 1944, when I was conceived. I remember nothing before then. I was, if I care to accept Seneca's way of looking at things, dead. I had been dead for millions of years – forgive me, I'm poor on the precise maths – until Richard and Esther, of Bonnybridge, Scotland, decided they wanted a child. I was thus raised from the dead without anyone asking my permission, brought forth out of the womb into a state of being called alive; or, anyway, of no longer being dead. I shall soon be restored to my former state, dead once more. End of story. What more of human existence need be said when Seneca said it all two thousand years ago?

Except this. I believe it may have occurred to you already, even if it appears not to have occurred to Seneca. The first death fails to qualify, misses the cut by miles, because it is unassociated with sensation of any kind. For the millions of years we were dead, we had felt no pain, no love, no anger, no ambition, no altruism, no selfishness, no grief, no anything. There followed the brief interval of life – usual over-priced plonk in the crush bar, best order before the show starts – in which we did feel pain, love, anger, ambition, altruism, selfishness and grief, and no doubt all sorts of other stuff that escapes me at the moment because I'm distracted by the bleeping of a help button up the corridor.

It's finally stopped.

I've looked back over that last paragraph, but have decided that I don't want to add to the terrible weight of pain, love, anger, ambition, altruism, selfishness and grief, which are surely enough to be going on with. And so – I proceed to state the obvious, as we journalists do – our second death is quite different in quality because we must face it with a freight load of experience – that of the awareness of having lived.

Seneca was just playing with us and with words. I shall tell him so in due course, if I get half a chance.

I forgot to say, strange omission considering it was the main event of the day: I had another endoscopy at lunchtime. Two extremely jolly, talky nurses wheeled me down to the unit, in and out of lifts, along endless corridors, me in my pyjamas, a ludicrous spectacle, quite pitiable in its way, myself indifferent to the effect having quickly shed any residual inhibitions. The usual paperwork on arrival – my file is already competing with *War and Peace*

– and the usual question about whether any member of my family has ever been considered at risk of catching mad cow disease.

Doc X is waiting for me. A man of few words, most of them scary. Unsmilingly announces that I will be given a stronger local anaesthetic and stronger painkillers than last time. Ominous, but feel nothing thanks to Dr X's precision and skill. Afterwards, am returned to the patient area of the unit and told to lie flat and relax, which I drowsily do, before being conveyed back to the solitary bliss of my room at the far end of Station 9.

I'd been fasting in prep for that scope. Around 5 o'clock, Steven brings me macaroni, which I relish without ill-effect.

Saving copy at the end of each night in case I'm dead by the morning. In this line of work, you can't be too careful.

Saturday 6 October

A POOR NIGHT last night. Mind active. Then the peeing starts. Urine infection? The night nurse takes a sample, reports nothing untoward, reminds me of the amount of fluid they're pumping into me. On a drip from 9pm to 6am, with a refill at 3am. The wee small hours are difficult. The lonely, vulnerable time, when it's harder to escape the reality. The corridor is low-lit and deserted, the few staff unfamiliar. I follow the second hand of the clock, note the passing of each precious second, listen intently to its tick. Long to speak to a friendly voice, but all my friendly voices have closed down for the night. Even Miss F, the demanding patient in a neighbouring side-room, who issues peremptory instructions to the nurses in a manner reminiscent of Mavis Riley in *Coronation Street*, seems to have mislaid her script.

Around 2am, check to see if any Wi-Fi. None. The signal looks strong enough at times but access is frustratingly patchy. I pick up an email, then wait hours to pick up another, and replying is impossible.

Unaware of what is going in the world and no longer care. In *The Times* the other day, the edition that carried my piece, there was an image of perfect absurdity – Theresa May in her ill-advised trouser suit prancing onto the stage of the Tory conference, evidently to the accompaniment of an Abba track. *Waterloo*, I should think.

Is she still even prime minister? By the time we leave the EU on 29 March next year, three days after what would have been my 74th birthday, I'll be long gone. I'll never know if the country ground to a halt on Brexit Day, or if Nicola Sturgeon got her 'indyref2' (crass abbreviation) or if she won it, and I'll never know if Ayr United implausibly gained promotion to the Scottish Premiership. I should regret that I'll never know any of this and so much more. But the world of events, so preoccupying as recently as two weekends ago, has slipped away from me. It is no longer my concern. No news breaks for me, and all the headlines are closing ones.

Two weekends ago… how inconceivable that I was then more or less fully functioning. Don't do this. Don't start wallowing.

Deprived of sleep, I start thinking about a family photograph. There we are, the three of us – my sister

Linda, who is seven years younger, isn't in the picture – on the beach at Rothesay, on the Clyde island of Bute, where the urban working class used to repair *en masse* for a week in summer, long before the era of cheap continental travel, to a resort of Spartan boarding houses, sandcastles, music hall and unreliable weather. I don't have this photograph with me, but I have it embedded in my mind. My mother smartly turned out, smiling broadly, cute as any 1950s brunette cover girl. My father in his blazer, his heavily Brylcreemed hair slicked back, the plausible B-picture rogue, also grinning for the camera. Myself in shorts, but looking decidedly less happy, the obligatory smile gentle but guarded.

I was so solemn as a small child that my parents nicknamed me Gloomy Joe. Soon I was demanding a pen and paper for the purpose of recording what I saw and heard around me. What I observed could not have delighted me, for the gloom never quite lifted. It lingered well into adult life, and does so even as I prepare to leave the stage. My natural expression was a serious one, however hard I tried to lighten up. Sometimes strangers would be sufficiently concerned to inquire after my welfare. Once, in Pitlochry, outside the chip shop on Atholl Road, I was working for the BBC at the time and something of a minor celebrity, a woman accosted me in quite a challenging fashion. 'What have you got to be so miserable about?', she asked. 'Why can't you be as pleasant as Sandy Lyle?' After this unsettling episode I studied the form of the affable Lyle with some interest. It declined sharply for a while, and he too began to look fairly grim, though obviously not in the same league of world-class grimness as myself. But then, I noted, his tournament performances perked up, which was attributed to his new relationship with a Dutch physiotherapist who tickled his toes last thing in the evening. I should have worked harder at finding some equally ingenious solution. But it is too late now. Gloomy Joe will go to his grave as gloomy as the day he was born, toes defiantly untickled.

Still, it niggles: the Pitlochry Question. 'What have you got to be so miserable about?' What indeed? I'm putting it to the back of my brain and hope to get back to you.

The cruellest cut of all, a real killer this one: to awake from sleep and for a few moments imagine that it's the start of an ordinary day, a day of rude health and full of purpose. It hasn't happened yet, quite, but I can imagine that, if it did, it would be traumatic and destabilising.

Sunday 7 October

A RELATIVELY UNEVENTFUL NIGHT. Still hooked up to a drip, I manage to manoeuvre myself out of bed and over to the window. Sit there for a while with the window open. The fresh autumn breeze feels like oxygen. I don't have much of a view – only to another part of the hospital, offices they look like – but I can easily imagine the hills of Carrick, the sea, Ailsa Craig. How fortunate I've been to live in this part of the world.

So I am not quite bedridden yet. A walk of a few feet (none of the awful light-headedness of a week ago) is enough to give me a sense of achievement. In such tiny accomplishments do I measure – I was about to write 'my progress', but there's no progress nor any hope of progress

– so what I am measuring? At best, and gratefully, any tiny slowing of the relentless march.

Welcome to my room. I should have introduced you to it before. It's nothing special, but it's all mine. It's Room 310, Station 9. It has a separate bathroom – en-suite facilities if I'm being posh about it – the effect only slightly spoiled by two ugly signs on the bathroom door both marked 'TOILET'. Each is illustrated by a drawing of a toilet seat, a useful guide for the many patients who have no conception of what a toilet seat looks like.

I have come to realise that a person of limited mobility, detained in a confined space, develops an inordinate curiosity about objects just beyond his reach. I'd been wondering for ages about the contents of a Morrisons bag, so when Steven (lovely man; I don't know his title, auxiliary maybe) came in to say hi this morning I asked him to investigate. It contains a charger for my laptop, which, as it happens, is all that is left of the laptop for the time being.

After lunch yesterday – I should have told you this at the time – I was quite proud of having got through pea soup and a small fish pie and was looking forward to doing some work on this diary, when I discovered that the recently acquired Mac had packed up. Panic. I shut it down, rebooted, still kaput. My first thought: I've lost 3,000 words. I've never lost as many as 3,000 words before. My second thought: I'm too ill to start again. I dissolved and cursed my wretched fate. Bad enough to be dying. But I draw the line at a computer destroying 3,000 words.

Islay came; Islay knows about these things. She fiddled about with it for ages, staring intently into what appeared to the others in the room a black featureless screen. Only Islay was able to detect the faint outline of text. 'Were you writing about someone being grim?', she asked. 'Yes, yes,' I said. 'I was describing myself in relation to Sandy Lyle.' 'In that case,' she said, 'your piece is still here. I think I know what's happened. The bulb's gone.' We are now hoping that a computer repair company in Ayr will be able to replace the bulb and retrieve my 3,000 words first thing on Monday.

Meanwhile, I have a replacement laptop so that the posthumous masterpiece continues uninterrupted.

I was starting to tell you about my room and got no further than two lavatory signs of limited aesthetic merit and a Morrisons bag. There's a bit more to it than that. There is a side table that can be wheeled about. This morning on the side table we have three bottles for the discharge of urine, a plastic cup with a foul-tasting liquid that I swallow in instalments – they claim it is to improve my potassium level, and I have no reason to doubt it; I have a policy of never arguing with the medical profession – a beaker of water, a bottle of Lucozade, to which I'm addicted, my watch, my mobile phone and some paper towels.

In the far corner, there is a small cupboard full of diversions: books, CDs, films, a radio. I have little current use for any of it. Despite my assurance to the readers of the *Scottish Review* and *The Times* that I intended to occupy myself with a literary bucket list, I can't concentrate for more than a page or two. I did try listening to the radio and rather liked nodding off to *Gardeners' Question Time*, but that's about as far as I got with Radio 4, apart from stumbling on the news, which I instantly switched off. Like a character in a David Hare play, I don't approve of the news.

I started to watch a few films, but not with any enjoyment. Even one of my all-time favourites, *North by*

Northwest, didn't hold my interest past the opening scene in the Plaza Hotel – it was the Plaza, wasn't it? – where Cary Grant is held at gunpoint by a couple of mean hombres. I kept thinking that most of the actors in it, including Cary Grant and James Mason, are long dead and wondered how they managed with their dying. I just couldn't find a way past the death obsession thing. Also, it was painful to see seductive New York by night; it made too many connections with the pleasures of the past.

I suppose, too, I was plagued by the thought that listening to pleasant radio programmes about garden peas, or watching old movies, was a waste of the little that remains to me; I don't feel I have the luxury of 'passing time' in that profligate way the healthy take for granted. It is curious, maybe a bit pathetic, that the only compulsion I still possess is a creative one: to commit words to paper. Nothing has changed, then. I'm essentially the same Gloomy Joe whose only need in infancy was to have the implements of writing at his immediate disposal.

Back to room 310. On the other side of the bed I have placed two blue plastic chairs which have become an informal filing cabinet of essential supplies. On one of them is a sponge bag with toothpaste and toothbrush, a razor, a comb and a can of deodorant.

My designer stubble was coming along nicely, or so I thought until one of the auxiliary nurses said firmly that I didn't suit it and insisted on shaving it off. She did it without leaving a nick: most impressive. Yesterday I tried giving myself a shave, but that necessitated looking at myself in the bathroom mirror, which I hadn't done for nearly a fortnight, and I was so repelled by what I saw that

I cut my chin and gave up, retreating bloodied and shocked to the bed.

On the second chair I keep the current issues of *The Spectator* and the *New Yorker*, which Barbara brought yesterday. I'll have a go at those later, especially as I see from the teasers that Mary Wakefield has a piece in *The Spectator* about the vileness of cyclists, a subject on which Ms Wakefield and myself are in complete agreement. Also on the second chair, a fat file of emails in response to my valedictory editorial, a selection of which Islay intends to publish in next week's *Scottish Review*. I'm not going to say much about these emails; they are too overwhelming to contemplate at the moment. I am attempting to have a day without tears.

You will be sorry to hear that I am not quite done with the second chair. Its most vital asset is a box of Tesco Balm Extra Large Tissues ('Previously Called Mansize'), which is my best friend in the middle of the night in the case of accidental spillage from the pee bottle. If you don't like this talk about bodily function, skip to the next paragraph which I'll make more sweet-smelling, but this is a story about dying, and I've discovered that dying involves indignity, and there's no getting away from it. If a dying man's penis, at 3 in the morning, misbehaves in the process of discharging pee into a cardboard container, that is one definition of indignity. At that point, the owner of the penis is strongly advised to reach for a Tesco Balm Extra Large Tissue ('Previously Called Mansize') and wipe up the mess as best he can. The sensible strategy (I'm telling you this in case you end up in a similar predicament, and therefore for your own good) is to wear a pair of sturdy underpants under your pyjamas.

I think I've just about exhausted the contents of room 310, Station 9, so I'm off to have a squint at the *New Yorker*.

I'm back.

The listings in the *New Yorker* are a shadow of what they were. I went at once to the theatre section and was surprised to find only five plays mentioned, none of them on a mainstream Broadway stage. What gives? The weekly guide, crisp and urbane, used to be one of the glories of this publication and of New York life in general. And it isn't as if the selected five – so help me, five – sound all that great. Least of all did I like the sound of *Uncle Vanya* at somewhere called Hunter College, in which the actors are expected to deliver their soliloquies direct to members of the audience. More annoyingly, one of Chekhov's characters has been dropped, perhaps in some misguided cost-cutting exercise though just as likely as a result of directorial arrogance.

Oh dear, what would Young Fred have made of this sacrilege? Vigilant readers will remember Young Fred from a few pages ago as the son of my grandfather Fred by his second marriage to Mary (Schofield). Young Fred was an exceptionally bright boy, dux of Denny High School in the year I was born, and went on to Glasgow University, which few in Bonnybridge did. He then had the misfortune to be called up for national service in the Korean war, a terrible experience from which, I suspect, he never quite recovered. After it was over he tried to establish himself as a teacher somewhere in England, but found the work and the dreariness of 1950s provincial Britain stultifying, and decided to emigrate to America with the aim of establishing himself as an actor. Truth to tell he was no great shakes as an actor, even in Bonnybridge. But he lacked nothing in ambition, so off he went to New York.

In Manhattan, he rented an apartment in the same block as a young actor, Jack Nicholson, who was making a name for himself. Fred wasn't making a name for himself and was grateful for Nicholson's encouragement and occasional subs. Slowly he patched together a portfolio of small acting jobs, some teaching, and writing for magazines. He also started drinking heavily. He also got married.

By the time he sorted himself out, Fred – Greg Roy as he was known professionally – was no longer young or promising. The marriage didn't survive, but he kicked the booze and converted to Roman Catholicism, the faith of his mother Mary. His five seconds of fame came in an excellent film, *The Verdict*, with Paul Newman, in which he played the jury foreman. All he had to do was deliver the verdict – 'Not Guilty' – which he did in what sounded like an Irish brogue.

He corresponded regularly with my mother, who was always intrigued to hear about his latest adventures, but he returned to Scotland only once, when I was a young boy. My memory of the occasion is that a party was going on downstairs in our house, a loud party preventing sleep. There was nothing unusual about that: our house was party central. But then I heard feet on the stairs. And suddenly he was looming over me, the guest of the evening, the star from across the Atlantic, who had arrived after my bedtime: a glamorous figure, with his handsome square face and firm chin and American drawl. He asked me a question about *Tom Brown's School Days* and I couldn't answer it. I felt embarrassed by my ignorance. He returned downstairs and by the morning the party was over and the living room was full of empty bottles and there was no sign of Fred or his alter-ego Greg.

I didn't see him again for more than 40 years. I was in New York for Christmas and New Year, celebrating my survival from a near-fatal pulmonary embolism, and decided to invite him out for dinner. I did so with extreme hesitation because a few years earlier, when my son Stephen had a summer job in New York, he rang Fred and suggested a meeting. Fred made some excuse. I was shocked and upset by this slight and thereafter considered Fred a shit. But one night close to the end of my own New York trip, I thought what the hell and picked up the phone. We arranged to meet the following evening in the lobby of my hotel.

I watched him arrive. Puffy, a bit out of breath, carrying a lot of weight, well wrapped in a heavy overcoat, he looked older than his 60 years. Instant pang of nostalgic melancholy as I remembered the heady excitement of that Bonnybridge night long ago.

He glanced over at me. 'A Roy,' he said. 'Recognise a Roy anywhere.'

We trudged off into the freezing Manhattan night, to a smart restaurant called the Madison Bistro, where he immediately made a fuss of announcing that, of course, he wouldn't be drinking. The not-drinking was meticulously documented – he would tell my mother in his letters exactly how many years, months, weeks and days he had been off it – and he believed in spreading the good news. When the pudding arrived, he sniffed at it claiming to detect alcohol. The waiter assured him that it contained not a drop, on his mother's life not a drop, and Fred reluctantly agreed to have the blameless pud.

By then he had stopped talking down my father. Fred's detestation of daddy Roy was boundless, yet he had accepted my father's hospitality on the famous Bonnybridge night. I asked him repeatedly what it was about my father that he hated so much, but never received a coherent answer. It was as if I should know, that no elucidation was necessary.

I got him off the subject by asking what he was writing at the moment, often a handy ruse in an emergency, and he produced a number of manuscripts – poems and a one-act play – adding that he understood I was a publisher of some sort back in Scotland and that I should consider publishing his work or placing it with another publisher. I said that my firm didn't publish poems and one-act plays, that we were a reference publisher, really quite boring, but he kept pressing the point and finally I said that I would have a look at them and see what I could do.

'Can we expect you in Scotland sometime?' I asked as the evening drew to a close.

'Not until I've made it', he replied. I looked at him in more or less open-mouthed astonishment. He was serious. Had he too been exhorted to 'Be Somebody'?

It was unclear whether he had any source of income; there had been little talk of work. But Young Fred still thought he could make it. The American Dream in his case was still alive. The big break was just around the corner. It was never too late.

Until it happened, there was no question of a sentimental trip to the old country. Fred would return in triumph to Bonnybridge and people would gasp, 'My God, isn't that Greg Roy?', and there would be media interviews and a civic reception. If this wasn't possible because no-one had heard of Greg Roy, the shame of failure would be too much to bear and the thought of exposing that failure unthinkable.

On the overnight plane home, I read the play. It was a two-hander, intense and verbose, about a father-daughter relationship. It wasn't bad and it wasn't good and there was no market for it, with the best will in the world no market. I couldn't decide if there was any merit in the poems; I am no good with poems. By the time we touched down in Glasgow, I'd resolved not to inflict any more humiliation on Fred; unlike the foreman of the jury, I wouldn't be delivering a verdict. We never corresponded or spoke again.

A couple of years later, Fred was found dead in his apartment in the middle of one of those punishing New York heatwaves. The church of which he was a devout member put on a fine service, with an elaborate programme full of tributes to Fred and including some of his poems. I considered attending, in the end didn't. But a week or two later, a courier in Irvine, where I was based at the time, attempted without success to deliver a brown parcel to my office: without success because the building was closed that day. I learned later that the courier promptly returned the parcel to the sender at an address in New York. It was then re-addressed back to Irvine, where it finally arrived, having crossed the Atlantic three times. I opened it, and Fred's ashes spilled out over the floor. I called for help from Fiona, and we scooped them up as best we could. Not at all sure what to do next, I took them to a family burial plot with a good view of the Grangemouth oil refinery, and put them next to those of my father, whom Fred loathed so much, and there they lie together for eternity or until the Grangemouth oil refinery blows up. So Fred did return. In fact, he returned twice in a week.

I had hoped for a day without tears. Not quite achieved. Margaret visited in the afternoon and we had a good greet together, which we agreed later was therapeutic and overdue. She brought a copy of today's *Herald*, which has a lovely piece about me by Ron McKay.

10.25pm. Christine, not to be confused with Stornoway Christina, has just been in for a chat. She tells me she is getting married next year and that the weather has turned nasty, with a storm warning for tomorrow. She asks what I'll do when I leave hospital and I reply honestly that I intend to go on writing until I drop. She nods, approvingly I think.

Here is a night terror: something I truly dread. The scenario (think I touched on it in passing a few pages ago): I wake up and think everything is all right; for a few moments I imagine that an ordinary day stretches ahead, a day full of purpose and plans. Then I remember. No more ordinary days. No more purpose. No more plans. Finis. It hasn't happened yet, but I rather fear it might, and it disturbs me because I know it would be upsetting, even destabilising. I can only exist in the reality of my situation, living from minute to minute, the clock ticking, hour by hour, the clock ticking, day after day, the clock ticking.

'We can't complain', I heard someone say today. 'We had such a good summer.' And I think: yes, my last, and I was bloody miserable for the whole of it. But I'm flirting with self-pity, the Roy failing. Stop.

I asked Steven to shut the window when the wind started to blow, rattling the blinds, so it's stuffy in here.

Hardly surprising if it's true, as one of the nurses said, that there are boilers above. And then there's the gentle noise of the drip (wired up for another night), which sounds like soft insistent rain. I think every night it will lull me to sleep, that and the sleeping pill, yet somehow I end up tossing and turning for hours.

Monday 8 October

WAKE UP – or rather am wakened by the arrival of day shift – around 7.30am feeling horribly weak and low. One of the auxiliaries, Pat, breezes in singing *Fly Me to the Moon*. I propose that we fly there together and she agrees. 'Do you know anyone on the moon, Kenneth?', she asks. 'Of course,' I assure her. 'Who?' 'The man.' 'What man?' 'The man on the moon, silly.' First laugh of the day. There may not be many more.

Next visitor: Hazel, the ward sister. Wonders what kind of weekend I had, and the discussion turns to my discharge. I tell her we have a plan in place: a ground-floor apartment with all the facilities close to each other and good people looking after me, but they're anxious to know what help we can expect. She utters reassuring noises: I am not to worry about that. So, for the moment, I don't. I trust Hazel implicitly. She is a good person.

Today, a grim anniversary. It was a week ago today that the firing squad arrived with the results of all the tests. I was still in a ward then, but they drew the curtains to give us some privacy. Five – or was it four? – stood at the head of the bed facing me. Dr X, the head honcho, spoke first;

maybe he was the only one to speak. Expressions uniformly solemn.

Dr X didn't waste words. There was no prospect of surgery. The tumour was inoperable. The internal bleeding would be difficult to stop, though he would try to minimise it. At some stage, as the passageway narrowed, he would fit a stent to widen it, but the day would come when I could no longer eat or drink. If I wanted to consider palliative chemotherapy or radiotherapy, he could facilitate this, but it would mean daily trips to Glasgow. I said – it was my first contribution – that I didn't fancy daily trips to Glasgow and that I didn't see the point anyway. Dr X did not demur.

'The prognosis?'

He said that with cancer it was always difficult to predict. 'But' – he was about to predict it anyway. I watched with horrid fascination to see the word that would form next on his lips. The word was 'months'. I don't think I responded other than to thank him for being so frank. Someone asked me if I had any questions. I said that I couldn't think of any.

I did half-think of asking what my chances were of having to sit through another Hogmanay show. I decided against. It might have struck a note of inappropriate levity.

One of them reopened the curtains, relieving the unbearable claustrophobia. The man in the bed opposite, 'The Smoker' as I call him, who might have heard every word, was still hacking his lungs off. Dr R, who visited him briefly one day, asked to see his hands. 'Twenty a day on this hand,' he said. 'Twenty a day on the other.' The Smoker boasted to anyone who would listen that, as soon as he got home, the first thing he would do was light a cigarette. His nebuliser kept the ward awake long into the night. By the end of my stay there, I had formed a not altogether irrational dislike of The Smoker.

As I digested the extraordinary information I had just received, reflecting on my new status as a condemned man, the firing squad moved off and a few seconds later they were at the far end of the ward chatting amiably with another patient. There was the sound of laughter from the corridor.

Nothing had changed. The scene looked exactly as it had 10 minutes before. There was no indication that the earth had moved. After a few minutes, I reckoned I'd better contact family and colleagues and give them the news that no-one had been expecting. No-one, that is, but me. In my own mind there had never been the slightest doubt. Not for months. I'd always suspected that my body would do the dirty on me and knock some time off for bad behaviour. This was mere confirmation.

I have no memory of the state I was in when Fiona arrived from the office, but the first thing she did was seek out the ward sister (we didn't know her as Hazel till later) and request a side room. What seemed like minutes later, I was moved to one, and I've been here ever since.

3.30pm. I've just been visited by one of the junior doctors, who took blood, and we chatted about Unst, where she lived for a while as a child. I asked if anything was happening on Unst (if you're unfamiliar with it, it's the farthest point of the British Isles). She pulled a face and said the bar at Baltasound had closed. I remember it as rather a nice little bar run by a colourful woman called Mavis, who sported a poncho. No more, it seems.

Earlier the dietician called, dishing out leaflets about what I should and shouldn't eat when I leave hospital. I am to go for broke and avoid low-fat anything. 'Eat little and often,' she counselled. Suits me. Oh, and a nurse from palliative care, who wondered if I'd need a stick or even a zimmer frame on my departure. I said it was all too probable the way I was feeling, assuming I could get out of bed at all.

It emerges that I am to be put in the care of the social services – could I ever have dreamt I'd end up as a 'case'? – which will attend to my post-hospital needs. Oh, the damnable indignity of it all. Talking of which, in the small hours of the morning, reaching out for a glass of water in the dark, I spilled more or less the entire contents of a pee bottle over the bed. Christine was an angel and within minutes I was restored to clean sheets. But the decline in my functioning power is indeed devastating.

The visiting is in full swing. No one for me until later. Islay was here again this morning sorting out another computer problem – I'd succeeded in losing a further 3,000 words on the replacement laptop but she managed to recover them somehow. She is a genius with machinery and never loses her cool. The computer repair shop in Ayr has taken my own laptop in for repair; the first 3,000 words should be returned no later than Thursday. But is someone up there trying to tell me something?

I've been sleeping more than usual today. Can begin to see the shape of an ending: 'making him as comfortable as possible'.

And thinking of the past; for the dying, there's always the past to try to make sense of. Poor Fred. Was I unfair to him? He so longed for fame; how life must have disappointed him. From the same New York address that despatched the ashes, I received a handwritten book of quotes he'd compiled, a copy of Catherine Carswell's *The Life of Robert Burns*, heavily annotated, and a diary for 1993, the year he died. I couldn't find any record of social engagements – not so much as a visit to the cinema – or work assignments; only prompts about dry cleaning (something of a preoccupation with his pants) and an underlined entry marking the anniversary of the day he gave up the booze.

The only reason I've mentioned Fred again – you understand, I hope, that I can't do much about the clumsy construction of this document – is pure expedience. Through Fred, I want to get to my mother.

To the end his affection for my mother was undimmed. He regarded Esther Roy as a great unheralded talent of the stage. It was just her rotten luck to be landed with such a waster as my father.

She was born Esther Bernard, her surname hinting at possible French ancestry. And there was indeed a family legend that the Bernards arrived at the port of Grangemouth as supporters of Bonnie Prince Charlie, and that when the colossal misadventure failed, they settled in Scotland. I was never interested enough in this unlikely tale to look into it, but my mother was prepared to give it credence. Her extensive researches into the family tree failed to turn up any evidence.

She was the daughter of an engineer, Thomas Bernard, and his wife Isabella, and they had, as well as my mother Esther, a son George, and two other daughters, Isobel and Peggy. The family migrated to Bonnybridge from industrial

Lanarkshire when my grandfather landed a job as manager of one of the local works. It was an important job and it came with a valuable perk: the tenancy of Bonnyside House, one of the grandest houses in the district, a Gothic pile reached by a long drive overhung by trees. It was there that my mother was born in 1918.

The garden of the house bounded the Antonine Wall and the children enjoyed an idyllic existence playing where Romans had once laboured. But in 1931, when my mother was 13 years old, a triple calamity struck the family. Her beloved older sister Peggy, to whom she was devoted, died in a flu epidemic, just as my paternal grandfather's wife had in an earlier one, and in the same year her father Thomas lost his job after a falling out with the board of directors. He not only lost his job; he also lost the tied house.

He decided to seek work in London, and with that ostensibly in mind set off one evening to catch the train to Edinburgh from Greenhill Station, close to Bonnyside House. My mother watched sadly from her bedroom window as he trudged down the drive out of sight, and was still at the window when, to her delight, she saw him return. 'Daddy!', she cried. My mother believed it might have been at that precise moment – the supernatural sighting – that her father fell to his death under a train at Greenhill. Accident or suicide? It was never spoken of again, but there was a suspicion, perhaps even an assumption, that it was the latter.

Evicted from Bonnyside House, the widow and three surviving children secured lodgings in the village, and life for my mother was now far from idyllic. But she landed on her feet, as did her brother George, when a kindly local industrialist and Scottish patriot, John Rollo, proprietor of the St Andrew's Engineering Works, hired both of them. My mother was Rollo's secretary for many years, while George became his works manager. Esther might have further improved her prospects if she had done the sensible thing and married the local doctor. Instead, she fell for my father, who was better-looking.

Richard and Esther met through the local drama club, the Bonnybridge Players, where they were cast as the romantic leads. Only on stage was it a marriage made in heaven; the rest was hell. Esther, like so many young women before and after her, made the fatal error of deluding herself that she could 'change' her man. Surprise surprise, Richard went on drinking, impervious to reform or the increasingly desperate entreaties of his young wife.

When I was old enough to comprehend what was going on in the fractious household, the night I dreaded most was Friday. Friday was pay day, and in those days the workers received their pay in cash, in brown envelopes. My father invariably arrived home late on a Friday, sometimes very late, and I could sense my mother's seething exasperation. When he did turn up, there was no need for Esther to rip open the brown envelope. It had been opened hours earlier, and some of its precious contents – the family revenue for a week – squandered in the pub. My father felt it was nothing less than his due, his pocket money. My mother disagreed. The furious recriminations, which had a tedious circular quality, continued long after I crept up to bed. Friday was a sleepless night.

My father had a succession of jobs, and at one time ran a little shop, what would nowadays be called a convenience store. How the money was raised for that misguided venture I never discovered, and it duly flopped. Only the patronage of John Rollo kept us afloat.

And then I added to my mother's misery.

When I got my first job, as a junior reporter on the *Falkirk Mail*, my mother was overjoyed. It meant there would be a third brown envelope in the house on Friday. But I'd misunderstood the terms. The paper's owner, Mackie, had said during the interview, 'Expenses okay?', and I'd replied that I was sure the expenses would be in order.

Like an obedient son, I went home at the end of my first week and handed an ominously thin, but intact, brown envelope to my mother. Her shock was palpable: 30 shillings. Mackie was indeed paying expenses, my bus fare from Bonnybridge to Falkirk, but that was all he was paying. It didn't matter to me. I was just delighted to have had a break into journalism. I would have done the job for nothing. I'd have crawled to work if it would have saved Mackie the bus fare. But my poor mother's dream of some improvement in the family finances had been shattered, and I felt guilty at having let her down.

I got out of the house, and Bonnybridge, as soon as I could – I had just turned 18 when I left for Greenock.

Although I was now working in a bustling seaport and shipbuilding town on the west coast, far from Bonnybridge, and anxious to establish myself in the company of the cynics who worked for the *Greenock Telegraph*, I couldn't shake off my parents. My over-protective mother insisted on accompanying me to find what she regarded as 'suitable' digs when I would have preferred to make the choice myself; so I found myself living with an unprepossessing middle-aged couple on a council estate in Port Glasgow, far from the office and the attractions of Greenock.

At the first opportunity, I ditched the middle-aged couple and went to live in the spare room of a woman who kept pornography under my bed. I was too virginal and insecure to find it arousing that I was sleeping on top of a stash of well-thumbed erotica ideal for a young man's fantasies. As soon as I'd fixed up somewhere else to go, I left the week's rent on the table without bothering to make my excuses. I had been in Bonnybridge too long; I had no sense of adventure; there was no part of me that wanted to be seduced by the landlady.

My mother would not have made such an error. She would have looked under the bed before signing any tenancy agreement.

The interference of my father was in a different class: it filled me with embarrassment and shame. One day without telling me he came down to Greenock and introduced himself to the reporters; I happened to be on holiday that week. He invited one of the older reporters, Dick Smith, out for a drink – which Dick ended up paying for – and attempted to borrow money. I can't remember if Dick coughed up, but news got back to the office that my father was a menace to be avoided. My colleagues were tactful about it, but the experience was personally lowering.

His fragile life disintegrated. I told my mother that I couldn't bear to hear any more about him or his increasingly desperate misadventures, and for a while I was estranged from both of them.

My father was never nicer than when he was dying. He summoned David, my brother-in-law, and myself to Falkirk, where my parents had been reduced to living in a primitive council flat without bath or shower, escorted us to the nearest pub (the Roman Bar) and announced over large whiskies that he would soon be dead and that we were to be sure to look after mum. He took to reading Steinbeck (*The Grapes of Wrath*) and developed something of a fictional gift of his own, claiming that the Falkirk postman – not sure which one – had found the secret of the holy grail.

He died in a tiny bedroom at home while my mother was briefly out of the room. His funeral was larger than anticipated. A number of men in black suits turned up and when I asked who they were, I was told that they were fellow members of Lodge Dolphin, Bonnybridge. Once a mason...

My mother, then in her late 50s, took naturally to widowhood and was happier than she had been since her childhood playing among the Roman remains. The terrible stress of living with my father had been lifted. She had her freedom at last, enjoyed it with continental holidays, and lived independently until near the end, when she entered sheltered accommodation in Colinton, Stevenson country, to be near my sister Linda.

While she was still able, we met regularly for tea in the lounge of the Caledonian Hotel. There hadn't been many hugs over the years, not many at all; Esther had not been the most demonstrative mum in the world. But we were probably closer in the anonymity of a hotel lounge than we had ever been in the intimacy of unhappy domesticity. Still, though, she didn't hug me; and still I didn't hug her. There was a reticence, an awkwardness. Never tall, she had been diminished by osteoporosis and, after we walked painfully slowly together out of the hotel, and I'd accompanied her across Lothian Road, she insisted on continuing alone to the bus stop. She never turned back.

Did I feel love for her? I never came closer than I did watching her cross the short distance that separated us in Lothian Road. For all her life she had been severely practical – she'd had to be to keep her family afloat; just as there had been few hugs, there hadn't been a great deal of laughter. But the indomitability of the woman: it was impressive.

In the week of her death, at the age of 87, she rang me. 'Kenneth,' she said, 'I am just calling to say that you have been a very good son.' I didn't have time to reply before she hung up. A few nights later, a carer found her body in a walk-in cupboard. She had opened a box of family heirlooms and was clutching a piece of jewellery.

One curiosity of her funeral at Mortonhall Crematorium on a hot July day was baffling and upsetting. The service was conducted by the minister of Colinton Parish Church, of which she'd long been an active member, and one supposes that the man got to know her reasonably well over the years. Yet there was no mention of her renown in Falkirk as a gifted amateur actress (if not quite the Ellen Terry of Fred's imagination). He said instead that she was well-known in Colinton for her singing, which was news to me and perhaps to others. I didn't have an opportunity to correct him, for within seconds of the service ending, he was off to his next gig. My mother deserved better than this perfunctory send-off.

My last conscious thought tonight is of Larkin's tribute to parenthood, the line about your mum and dad fucking you up. It's too glib. Most of us do a reasonable job of fucking ourselves up. I'm not going to claim that I was fucked up by my father and mother who had been dealt tough hands in childhood. I made my own life. I prevailed, after my fashion.

Tuesday 9 October

PROBABLY THE BEST night's sleep since I arrived here – and with a jolt I realise that it was a fortnight ago today. 'Pulse faint,' noted the ambulanceman. 'You need fuel.' As soon as we arrived at the hospital, I was taken to a large single room – I was struck by its whiteness – and pumped with blood and fluids round the clock. '15 min obs,' I heard someone say. I was told I was in an assessment centre. And for several days – I have forgotten how many – I was rarely left alone. How they ministered. How they monitored. Ceaselessly. Devotedly.

I used to be a believer in angels, guardian ones. For years I was convinced I had my very own. I could think of no other explanation for my survival of what should have been a fatal air accident at Biggin Hill. Recently, though, I no longer sensed his (or her, or its) presence. I think my guardian angel decided I'd been rescued from one scrape too many and buggered off. Now I have the angels of the NHS. I find them more dependable.

One morning I was surprised to receive a visit from a consultant at 7.30am. 'I didn't know you guys were up and about at this hour,' I said. He introduced himself as Dr R and explained that he didn't sleep much beyond 5am and might as well be at work. We chatted for a bit, and he said he had an open mind about what was wrong with me. A stomach ulcer, he speculated. They would do some tests and get a better idea.

Next time I saw him, they'd done the tests and discovered a large tumour between the oesophagus and the stomach. No prognosis, though. There was still a glimmer of hope that it might be treatable, if not exactly shown the door, even if the expression on Dr R's face told a different story. His parting shot was that I would now be assessed by the surgical team. That was my last little chat with Dr R. Pity. He had a lovely voice for imparting bad news.

A couple of days later, in the late afternoon, a nurse came hurriedly into my room and announced that I was being transferred to 'Gastro' ward under the care of the surgical team.

'When?'

'In 15 minutes,' she said with an air of urgency.

The abruptness of the move – from the cosseted solitude of my quarters in the assessment centre to a busy ward – was disorientating. My initial sensory impression of 'Gastro' was of a modern version of Bedlam. A demented old man, feet away, was howling uncontrollably. He continued to howl all night. Another patient was swearing at the nurses. I texted a friend at 3.30am – how bloody selfish of me – to say that there was no peace and no dignity in my new existence; that I'd rather be dead. Fortunately she didn't pick up the message until the morning.

And by the morning, the old man had gone. I asked what had happened to him, but the nurse gave an evasive answer. He was replaced later that day by a 92-year-old, in excellent shape and with all his marbles, who gave no trouble and spent most of the day reading *The Herald* – he offered me the sports supplement when he'd finished with it – and doing puzzles. But then there materialised The Smoker, to whom I alluded earlier, who was on an oxygen mask or a nebuliser for hours every day. I tried speaking to him once and got a grunt in reply, which seemed to say: fuck off.

My visitors made every attempt to help me block out the horror: all manner of heavy duty ear plugs, a radio with dodgy reception, even an eye-mask. The accessories helped a little, but the assault on the senses was too overpowering to be completely eradicated. A long, nasty fluorescent light on the ceiling didn't tend to be switched off until 11pm or later, and even then the ordeal of the night lay ahead with its hideous cacophony of snores and groans and writhings.

The relief at being given a side room is barely describable. Nicola Sturgeon, when health secretary, was right to defy the medical profession and insist on a single room for most patients at the big new hospital in Glasgow. If her public service amounted to nothing more than that single humane decision, her political career would be justified.

12noon. Dr X calls in on his ward rounds.

'Bowels just moved?' is his opening gambit.

'Sadly, no, I just farted. Sorry about the smell.'

There is nothing very new to report: outlook grim. I am the Albion Rovers of Station 9. But then he lets slip that there's a consultant at Crosshouse Hospital who might be prepared to give me laser treatment. Should he speak to her? 'Sure,' I say.

He is going on holiday to India. We shake hands on the understanding that we probably won't be seeing each other again.

'Fingers crossed,' he says as he leaves. So it comes down to that.

Also this morning, a visit from physio Rose. 'Have you been walking much?', she asks.

'Hardly at all, being hooked up to machines most of the day and night.'

She produces a stick and asks if I'd like it. I accept.

'Then let's see you on your feet.' I struggle out of bed and stagger as far as the bathroom unaided, and then back to bed with the help of the stick. I hit the pillows exhausted, but bubbly Rose seems delighted.

Lisa (auxiliary nurse) pops in from time to time. I love her cropped red hair and her unaffected good humour. She lives in the village of Dalrymple where my old friend Iain Cuthbertson spent his final days. Until the step-up three months ago, she worked in the hospital kitchens. I'm disappointed to hear that she has no ambitions to be a nurse. She would make an excellent nurse.

Lunch (it seems no time at all since breakfast): I finish off some pasta. Christina declares that my blood pressure has dropped a bit and asks if I've been drinking enough. Like a good boy I reach for the Lucozade.

Another morning over. Visitor due at 2pm. How quickly one becomes accustomed to the daily routine, the abject dependence, the bleep-bleep of buzzers, the rattle of trolleys, the weather updates (the rain has just stopped), the cheery chatter of the auxiliaries. To some I am 'darling', to others 'son', to Steven and Brian I am 'pal'. I am already institutionalised, and there is a part of me that likes it and fears re-entry into the outside world.

I think of a friend who made wrong calls in her youth, and served two years of a four-year sentence for drug offences. In the final stretch at Cornton Vale prison, she had a job in Stirling Library and returned after work to a house in the grounds, where her fellow inmates included some of the most notorious women in Scotland. She discovered that even murderers could be nice people. When release loomed, she didn't want it. She was terrified to lose the security and stability.

There is a little bit of me that feels the same. The hospital is one enormous comfort blanket. Remove it, and how long do I have? I am choosing not to think about it. Of course I'm thinking about it. At a meeting this afternoon with a palliative care nurse, it was agreed that, for all sorts of practical reasons, discharge before the end of this week is out of the question, that realistically we are talking about next Monday. I was asked if I would mind waiting until next Monday, and I tried not to sound too keen about next Monday when the truth is that I love the idea of next Monday.

So next Monday it is. Maybe.

5.10pm. Yet another meal has been served to my table. For many months I could scarcely eat a thing. Now my appetite has been restored to some extent, and Dr X assures me that the passageway is 'wide'. What did I order? I lift the lid. Macaroni.

6.20pm. It's stuffy in here, so I ask them to leave the door ajar and the window open to create a through draught. The gulls are circling the building opposite, and they don't sound happy. Tick-tock, time passes. What do I do with the rest of my evening? M and I used to do the crossword together, but I don't like doing crosswords on my own and, anyway, I don't have any newspapers.

Tick-tock, time passes. Christina pops in to say she's almost at the end of her shift and won't see me again until Friday. Sound of bins being emptied. The wind's up again, but they say a mini-heatwave is on the way. Autumn. I must make the best of it. It used to be my favourite season, when everything got going after the madness of summer, but if you're facing your last season it doesn't matter much what season it is. Ah, a visitor: a young cleaner with an itchy nose. 'Could be a sign you're annoyed,' I suggest. 'I am annoyed,' she said. 'What about?' 'I'm annoyed with my boyfriend.' Tick-tock, time passes. And I'm still severely constipated; there are times when I think of little else but how to shift the shit. Christina has given me one more shot with a strong laxative. If that fails we're looking at an enema tomorrow. I wasn't sure what that involves, so I asked Hazel earlier. More indignity but I'm not bothered. She added the interesting information that as long as I'm farting freely, things aren't too bad in that department. Now I'm checking the number of pee bottles I have for overnight use: somehow or other I have acquired five. I don't get a lot of warning, so I have them strategically placed for easy access. Surprised to find that I've used up almost an hour on that paragraph. Tick-tock, time passes.

Miss Brotherston. It was years and years later that I discovered her first name was Elizabeth, and the only reason I found out was that I happened to mention her as a positive influence in my life in a newspaper column. She wrote back to say that she had followed my career with the greatest interest, never missed an article of mine, and that she was now living quietly in retirement in the Borders. I replied that it would be lovely to see her again. An empty sentiment: we never met and the correspondence fizzled out. But I continued to think of her, and I am thinking of her tonight, probably for the last time.

She was a tall, elegant young woman with immensely striking jet black hair. I may have been a little in love with her when she was my primary 5 teacher. I wanted to please her and was mortified if I didn't. She taught me about the beauty and utility of words, their flexibility and their power, as well as instructing me in the mechanics of sentence construction, spelling and punctuation. I don't remember her teaching me anything else. We were complicit in our love of language. The rest was immaterial.

I was so eager to impress Miss Brotherston that I turned in an essay – although it may have been called a composition – using fancier words than usual. I had plundered the dictionary for words that I imagined would delight her. One of them was 'conflagration'.

For once, she was not delighted.

'No need to use big words, Kenneth, when small words do the job just as well. What was wrong with fire?'

There was nothing wrong with fire. I never used the word 'conflagration' again. But how lucky was I to have such a teacher? She saw something in me, some raw talent for the written word, and devoted herself to developing and encouraging it. Are there still teachers like her? Is the spirit of Elizabeth Brotherston alive? It seems to me the most important question you could ask about modern Scotland.

It's a quiet night on Station 9. One of the auxiliaries has just delivered a cup of strong black tea. I may not see anyone again until the morning, unless they come to check my BP (always on the low side) or stick a pin into my arm.

I am left alone with my thoughts; and, alone, I see there's a deeper significance in the story I've just told you about Miss Brotherston.

Gloomy Joe was never less gloomy – I wouldn't go as far as to say 'happier'; that would be pushing it – than he was at primary school. Whatever was going on at home, mum and dad could never fuck me up as long as I had the blessed distraction of school. Yet I shudder to recall the hierarchical system. Classes were big – around 40 – and arranged in strict order of academic attainment. Thus the boy who was consistently first in the class, Jim Lawrence, who went on to become a surgeon in Dumfries, occupied the furthest away seat in the back row. As the runner-up, I had the seat next to him, then the third-placed pupil next to me, snaking all the way down, row after row, to the seat under the teacher's nose reserved for the class dunce. It was appalling and it was cruel, but that is how it was and no-one questioned it in 1950s' Scotland.

9pm, and I'm not alone after all. Cheryl, the night nurse, has just arrived, and has heard about probable Monday release. 'Something to aim for,' she says. 'Yes,' I assure her with bogus enthusiasm.

Speak to M on the phone and ask how she's doing with the crossword on her own. Not well; having to look up a lot of answers. We're both having to look up a lot of answers now, one way and another.

Then a brief chat with Islay about tomorrow's *Scottish Review*. She says that the only way she could cope with setting the readers' letters about my forthcoming demise was to pretend that it was someone else. I've read them all now, the ones she's selected for publication, and the majority for which there is no space. I can't talk about them. Maybe later. If there is a later.

Only one of the many messages unsettled me. It was from a Church of Scotland minister and didn't refer to me at all. It consisted of two quotations from scripture. I didn't find them comforting. If there is a God, I hope to God he's a more personal one.

End of the day (9.40pm) and the usual nauseous taste in the mouth. Twice last night I feared I might throw up. The buzzer by the bed is my lifeline. Press it, and someone comes running. What they don't come running for is the pay.

Wednesday 10 October

5PM. I HAVEN'T BEEN ABLE to do anything with this diary today. I felt so bunged up first thing that, after breakfast, which I didn't eat, I asked to see Hazel and she suggested she perform an enema at once. She fetched a commode and then she and Lisa rolled me over on my side and began the procedure. I was told to 'keep them in as long as possible'. It didn't seem long at all before I was evacuating into the commode big time.

I fainted. 'Failed to respond,' as Hazel put it. They pressed an emergency buzzer, summoning doctors. When I came to, I was looking at the concerned face of one of the junior doctors. Lisa said later that I wasn't out for more than a few seconds, but the fact that 'the episode' happened at all is disturbing.

They got me back into bed and I sank gratefully into the pillows. The phone kept ringing with news of Ian Jack's page-long piece about me in *The Guardian*, and Fiona arranged for a copy of it to be sent to my room, but I felt too ill to look at it. Rest of the morning in and out of sleep, incapable of thought or action.

No memory of the evening, then a definitive moment in the early morning: I vomit sinister black coffee grounds over the floor. I've seen this before: it's dried blood from my stomach.

Terror in the night: I don't have months. Dr X, he of the crossed fingers, was being tactful. He could not have been crossing them firmly enough. I have – what – hours? Days? Surely no more. At 2am, I'm aware of the presence of a junior doctor – how good-looking they all are – and he says they're going to give me a unit of blood, maybe two. I ask him what is likely to happen, and he talks about moving me to Crosshouse Hospital for the laser treatment. I reply that I am happy here and don't want to die in some old man's ward in Kilmarnock. He nods sympathetically. Don't remember much about the rest of the night, apart from the occasional spasms of mental agony.

Thursday 11 October

FIRST THING I TEXT M and the inner circle: 'Still here.' It's all I can manage.

Cheryl is day nurse. A good start to the day after the hideousness of yesterday. She is realistic, for which I'm grateful. No bullshit. Then I have a frank chat with Hazel. Was she surprised by the drastic turn of events? She wasn't. The treatment I'd had she called a 'quick fix', easily undone given the gravity of the problem. We discussed options: (1) Crosshouse, emphatically no; (2) going home, no, we both agreed that I would need round-the-clock professional care; (3) the local hospice, a marvellous place by all accounts, but tight for beds; (4) staying here to the end, being cared for by this amazing bunch of people, some of whom I have come to regard as friends, emphatically yes.

Steven gives me a wash and changes my bed. We talk a bit about films. 'Who's the most famous person you ever interviewed?', he asks. After a think I reply 'David Niven'. Steven, who was born in 1989, has never heard of David Niven, but assures me he's going to google him. I refrain from telling him that, three minutes before we went live on air, Niven coolly asked if he could change into a fresh shirt.

Then a meeting with Dr Gillen, to whom I warm at once. I confide in him my guilt that I am taking up a bed in an acute care hospital when I should be leaving the stage in some other theatre. He dismisses my concern in a kindly way and says it is a privilege to look after me, that he will do whatever he can for me – including further endoscopies to burn the infected area if I wouldn't find that too distressing. We discuss frankly the possibility, strong in my mind, that, when I feel I've had enough, I will give them the nod to switch off the machines: no more life-extending blood transfusions. He exudes not only a quiet, avuncular authority, but understanding and humanity. One of the junior doctors, Claire from Northern Ireland, who'd bought *The Times* with my article in it and personally delivered it to my room, tears in her eyes, is with the doc on his rounds, along with Hazel, who holds my hand tightly at one point.

In the afternoon, Barbara makes a five-hour round trip to see me and will arrive home in Colinsburgh in the dark. 'We're getting used to the idea of it now, aren't we?', I suggest, leaving the nature of the 'it' unspoken. We don't take it any further. We may have entered a phase in which much remains unarticulated, while being instinctively understood and accepted. Or not accepted. That's equally possible. More possible, even. Thinking ahead to a move to the hospice, an unlikely bet though it seems, Barbara enumerates the many virtues of those ultimate havens.

Because of the traumas of Wednesday, I omitted to mention that something nice did happen before the miscellaneous horrors unfolded: a visit from my sister Linda and my brother-in-law David. Linda was born at home and perhaps my most enduring childhood memory is of being gently ushered into my parents' bedroom and introduced to this mystifying bundle in my mother's arms. But the seven-year age gap meant that we lived largely separate lives as children. I did help her with her spelling, though, teaching her how to spell 'because', a word she struggled with. 'Think Beca, think use. Beca use.' It was always Beca use after that. Linda tells me she is with the Anne Frank Trust, which does much useful work in schools and prisons.

David, a retired teacher, is an Ayrshireman, from the once lace-making valleys, a man of personal warmth utterly without side. He cried. Linda said she was determined not to cry and almost succeeded. There was a lot of holding of hands.

Things unspoken. Why did I never have a candid conversation with Linda about our parents? Why do I not have one now? Would it help either of us or simply cause pain? Dying doesn't necessarily release inhibition; as I am finding, it can actually reinforce it.

I know she misses my mother keenly. Esther would have been 100 earlier this year. I texted Linda on mother's birthday to remind her. Of course, there was no need. Dear Linda. How I regret that we saw so little of each other. And regret, too, the hurt I may cause by opening or reopening wounds about our upbringing. But the past is all I've got now if I ignore the fast-diminishing present and I'm attempting, for me, a rare honesty about belatedly confronting that past.

I have finally read Ian's piece about me in *The Guardian*. It is typically thoughtful, beautifully crafted, with an unsurpassable ending, delicately touching on the profoundest questions of illness and death. He's sorry that, although we kept in regular touch, we hadn't seen each other for 25 years, when, I think, he was editing the *Independent on Sunday*. He has a holiday house on Bute and, as he occasionally suggested, we could easily have met on one of his trips, perhaps at Nardini's in Largs, but somehow, like so much else, it never happened.

I was amused to be told by Fiona of a phone call from Ian after the piece appeared making it clear that it was an errant sub who was responsible for the phrase 'fish place', when what Ian had written was 'fish palace', with its different meaning and resonance. If it's any consolation, the snow is no longer general over Ireland.

A gentle, erudite man is our Ian. When Professor Andrew Hook, emeritus professor of English literature at Glasgow University, said in a letter to me earlier this week that his favourite journalists were Ian Jack and myself, he couldn't have conferred a higher compliment.

Now I must own up to having committed a crime. I would have kept this confession until later in the narrative, but as I don't know how much longer I'll be 'around' – 'around', have I really resorted to 'around'? – I propose to give you it straight.

I did once boast to Fiona that I had a blameless record, that I had never knowingly broken the law. She corrected me, reminding me of the small matter of larceny at the Basil Street Hotel. The Basil was where I stayed during my once frequent trips to London; a place of Victorian high style, its corridors sumptuously furnished with antiques, its drawing room a sanctuary, its restaurant – no, nothing so common as a restaurant – its dining room, if you please, sparkling with fresh linen and deeply polished silverwear. A student from a London school of music played softly on the grand piano during dinner, but never so loud as to disrupt conversation. Adorable, adorable, in every way.

Sorry, I'm giving you a stop-over at the Basil before I turn to what I called my 'crime'.

I was a member of an exclusive club known as the Baselites. For a small annual subscription, the Baselites were entitled to rooms on a private floor of the hotel for a ridiculously low rate, which included a splendid English breakfast. There was only one drawback: the bedrooms on this floor had no bathroom or shower; you tramped along the corridor in your robes. Oddly, there never seemed to be any competition for the facilities. I began to wonder how many Baselites – or how few – there were.

One afternoon, when I was checking in, I heard a

familiar voice behind me. It was the Glasgow hard man turned sculptor and writer Jimmy Boyle.

Me: 'Jimmy! What are you doing here?'

Jimmy: 'Could ask the same question of yourself!'

He too was a Baselite. So that made at least two of us. But I began to pick up on rumours that the hotel was no longer making much money and that the two sisters who owned it (it had been in the same family ownership for all of its 90-year existence) were keen to realise the asset. I challenged one of the staff, who claimed to be the PR man, to confirm or deny. He pooh-poohed the speculation and said that the Basil was safe, entirely safe. A few months later it was put on the market.

I rang the manager and explained that I ran a charity for young people and that our courses and competitions necessitated the regular use of a bell. Would he consider donating the reception desk's bell to our charity as a memento of my favourite place in London? I got a brusque refusal. The bell was going. Everything was going. No exceptions.

On my next visit – my last before it closed – I extracted revenge. It was logistically impossible to steal the bell without being caught, but the long corridor to the dining room, with its alcoved writing desks, was deserted during the day and so I made my furtive way along it and sat down at a desk pretending to write a letter. When I left, it was with one of the wooden stationery holders. I took it back to Scotland, where it has been an office ornament ever since.

My office. I've just realised that I'll never see it again. I remember the last time only a few short weeks ago when I was still inhabiting the world of the normal. I'd foolishly decided to attend the Young Scotland/Ireland Programme at the Queensferry Hotel. I agreed to chair the opening debate (on drugs) and walked with some difficulty from my distant room to the conference centre. As the debate began, I felt light-headed but carried on somehow. I didn't go to all the sessions that week, but tried to eat, sometimes on my own, sometimes with a colleague, staying away from the formal dinners. On the final night I fled from the restaurant, nearly choking on an overcooked, late-delivered main course. Now that I know what I know, it shocks me to admit that I could easily have died there and then. We returned to the office and I took at once to the sofa. Fiona tried to interest me in a sandwich. I wasn't having any sandwich. I wasn't having much. Down the stairs of Liberator House, into Fiona's car, home, the beginning of the end. No more office. No more ordinary days. And, most sadly, no more Young Programme. North Queensferry was my 99th event in an unbroken sequence which began in November 2002. The century, which I'd promised would be my swan song, eluded me.

I asked Fiona when she called in after work how Islay was coping. She replied that Islay thought that the weaker I became the more I was transferring my strength to her. Some girl.

The clock, I've just noticed, is at the wrong date, an earlier one. So it's true: it really is later than you think. Literally true in my case.

Still haven't confessed my 'crime', the real one that didn't involve the Basil Street Hotel.

Lisa on her first obs of the night says my BP is 'low', but claims to be not overly concerned at this stage. I am terrified of a repetition of last night. My right hand shakes a little. All the fear seems to have been monopolised by the right hand, my writing one. I wonder if all us dying shake with fear. We? Us? No, it's us. Grammatical uncertainty to the end. I wrote in that *SR* piece, the farewell one, that when I was told I had terminal cancer I felt at peace for the first time in ages. But that was when I imagined I had 'months', which now feels like a luxury. Since then the months have shrunk to – I'm not going to finish the sentence. I refuse to bloody finish the sentence.

The low BP reading has put the wind up me. The long night may only be beginning, so postponing the crime confession feels like tempting providence. It's just gone 9pm and I'm tired, but here goes.

I was doing so badly at Denny High School, in my first year, that the report card, whose production I had been dreading, marked me close to zero in every subject. Even my love of English no longer counted for anything. I decided that I couldn't show my parents this shocking indictment, that I must find a way of maintaining the illusion that I was merely bog standard and not the worst-performing pupil in the class. I found a way. I stole another boy's report card. He had tested reasonably well. He would do nicely. With a bit of forgery – I forget the precise details – I passed it off as my own. Next morning, I showed my parents the fraudulent document and asked them to sign it. They seemed disappointed that I was not doing better.

If you consider the nature of the crime more closely, I was guilty of three offences: theft, defacing the property of the Stirlingshire education authority, and forgery. Later, when I came to report the affairs of Falkirk juvenile court, I had cause to reflect that boys guilty of much lesser offences were despatched to an approved school and to an improving regime of cold showers, endless physical jerks, and savage beatings with the sturdiest tawses.

What happened to me? The short answer is: nothing. I was neither questioned about it nor punished for it. But I had derived a shameful pleasure – or should that be shameless?; maybe both – from the act itself. I'd actually enjoyed committing such a deception and carrying it off so successfully. I decided that I had a criminal mind. I thought I wouldn't mind being a criminal, extemporising at the edge of society, knowing that I would constantly be flirting with prison, a threat or a promise that only added to the thrill.

I said the short answer was nothing. The short answer often is. But there is a longer answer to the story of the report card. It's just that it's late (10.30pm) and the longer answer is beyond me tonight.

Lisa seems slightly happier with the latest BP reading, but I remain in trepidation. How I dread the night hours, as all the dying must.

Word count: 11,901. If I can think of another 99 words, I'll have clocked up 12,000 on this file (the computer repair shop in Ayr cannot retrieve my first file of 3,000 words because the machine is so new they don't have the spare part: it must go back to the Apple store. Fiona going to Braehead at the weekend. Boring beyond belief, but some readers might be wondering). 42 words left to make target. Have texted the usual goodnights, texts back hoping I have a better night. But when each night could be the last, it's hard for any of us to say the right thing. 12,004.

Lisa again. Fitting a few hours of fluids. A serious girl.

'Are you okay, Kenneth?'

'Yes, I'm okay. Why do you ask?'

'Because you seem to be fidgeting a bit.'

It's true. I'm fidgeting a bit.

'The nights are the worst part, Lisa.'

'I know. But if you need me in the night – even if it's just for some company – press the buzzer, don't hesitate.'

She gives me the sleeping pill. It didn't help a lot last night, but you never know. One lives in hope. Except: one doesn't any more. One lives without hope. That is the essential thing about dying, unless you believe in God and all that, about which I am sceptical. You. One. Awful. Yet I'm disinclined to clean up the copy this late.

But if you are there, God – Big Man Upstairs, as my friend Ena Lamont Stewart used to call him – if you are, God, listen to me: I'm frightened. Scared shitless, if you must know.

11.30pm. I could feel the sleeping pill trying to sedate me, but the fear overcame the drug, so, having switched off Fiona's laptop for the night, it's back on again. This turns out to be fortuitous, as it coincides with the arrival of Liam, the ANP (Assistant Nurse Practitioner), who was also on duty last night during the vomiting incident, and we have a frank conversation about my disease and the certainty of further episodes. I tell him I'm trying to write a short (very short) book about dying, including reflections on the power of memory in the final days, and the need to achieve some internal resolution of the past, and we agree that the dying Tessa Jowell began a much-needed 'conversation' (as anything resembling a discussion seems to be called these days) on a surprisingly overlooked subject, surprising if only because it is ubiquitous, the one experience we all share once in our lives. Liam says he'd very much like to read the book and asks to see Ian Jack's *Guardian* piece.

After Liam goes, I feel a bit more composed for having spoken to him and drift into sleep around 1am.

Friday 12 October

A LOVELY HIGH-FAT YOGHURT for breakfast; I could have eaten two. Bubbly Lisa and Claire, my first visitors, in mischievous high spirits, bearing lunch menus and good cheer.

Steven is off for the next few days, so I insist on a shave before he goes. We chat about football. Evidently Scotland were beaten last night in Israel, in a new thing called the Nations Cup.

I'm on the phone when Hazel arrives and announces to my astonishment that they're taking me off the drip. What's going on? I am to drink as much as possible, keep myself hydrated, but no drip for the rest of the day.

'How you doin', kiddo?' texts my sister. Then Fiona rings with the news that David, our tech-savvy neighbour in Liberator House, an all-round good guy, has managed to retrieve the lost 3,000 words, which will soon be put on a memory stick, whatever that is, and be reunited with the present file to form a continuous narrative for the first time. I am overjoyed and tell David so.

Stornoway Christina, at the start of her day shift, has just heard that I won't be leaving. I assure her to her sad face that I am okay about it, more than okay, that I am reconciled, content. 'We don't think of you as a patient,' she says with heartfelt sincerity. 'We think of you as a friend.'

Feeling stronger than I have for a few days – how long will it last? I'm taking no bets – I'll attempt the longer answer I was banging on about yesterday, which is not an answer at all but a question, one that has troubled me all my life and troubles me still. How was a clever boy of 12, consistently second in class throughout his primary education, so disastrously unable to cope with secondary school? How did he end up leaving at the age of 15 with no qualifications?

Denny High School, which drew pupils from several neighbouring working-class towns and villages, including the paper-making town of Denny, specialised in institutionalised brutality: that, rather than the education of impressionable young minds, appeared to be the very purpose and core of its existence.

The system of creaming was spectacularly harsh. In that respect at least, Denny was not unique, merely conforming to Scottish policy and practice. The pupils were graded according to their final primary results in classes ranging from A for the brightest to H for the dimmest; and even the dimmest could claim to be part of an academic institution. For those considered beyond any conventional radar of dimness, the irredeemable no-hopers, there was the non-academic alternative of the junior secondary (Bonnybridge had one), where the curriculum relied on such practical skills as woodwork, which had the merit of preparing boys for useful employment but the obvious disadvantage of stigmatising them for life.

I was put in the A class at Denny along with Jim Lawrence and one or two others from Bonnybridge as the best of our village's intake. A glittering five years, followed by a place at Glasgow University to study English, should have been the outcome; might I even emulate Young Fred and have my name embossed on the roll of honour as dux of the school 1962, two Roys in 17 years?

I was immediately disabused. The first period on the first day of term was French, taught by a fearsome matron, Miss Riach. She entered the room in full dragon flow and was soon firing questions at her trembling subjects. I can't remember the first question, but, trying to make a favourable early impression, shot up my hand. It was the wrong answer, not very smart perhaps but hardly the crime of the century. Her withering look and sarcastic putdown, which I came to learn were her trademark qualities, made me feel like the stupidest person in Scotland. I'd left the gentle seminar atmosphere of Miss Brotherston's class far, far behind.

Almost incredibly – but then everything about Denny High in 1957 was in the realm of the almost incredible – Riach was not the worst. Miss Smith in mathematics may have been born into the world with hard, unrelenting features, a bitter tongue and an evil nature. I never heard her utter a kind or encouraging word to anyone.

Rather more than Riach, she derived a perverted delight, sexual in origin as I then didn't see, from applying her sinuous brown tawse to the outstretched hands of the boys, and on the flimsiest pretexts. We were ordered to cross our hands in a way that exposed the fingers of both, and after the first stroke, change hands for a second or third. On special occasions, driven to near-hysteria by our inability to grasp the simplest mathematical concept, she ordered all the boys down to the front for a mass belting, and we obediently queued up for our expertly administered stroke aimed viciously at the tips of the fingers, a ritual that must have absorbed at least five precious minutes of the time allotted for mathematics. This was not mathematics. This was the theatre of cruelty.

Although the failure to grasp the simplest mathematical concept was not gender-specific – the opposite sex had problems with numbers too – she spared the girls, presumably because her pyschosexual lusts were satisfied by boys alone. She was a disturbed person who was transparently unfit to be in charge of children. This should have been known to the authorities. Perhaps it was. But nothing was done about it.

The parents made no fuss whatever about the strange goings-on at Denny High School. On the contrary, they were mutely compliant, 'looking up' to such authority figures as the headmaster, the local doctor, and the parish minister. No one would have dreamt of complaining about Miss Smith, even when the stories of her alarming behaviour reached the home. The compliance was total, unchallenged, implicit.

Only once do I remember the use of corporal punishment being discussed. A group of neighbours, including my mother, sat together in the spring sunshine, and I was a silent onlooker, pretending to be doing something in the garden while straining to overhear.

'That new art teacher, the young one, belts the boys on the bum,' one woman said lightly.

'Is that allowed?', said another.

'No,' said the first, stifling a giggle, 'but she does it anyway, and I think the boys like it.'

The suggestion here was of a mutually beneficial experience, naughtily against the rules of course, but enjoyable for all concerned. Yes: the belt could actually be fun, a real turn-on, if the consenting parties were an attractive young female teacher and a class of nice-looking boys with no discernible talent for artistic expression but who got a kick from showing off their bums to a woman not much older than themselves.

Nothing was done about that either. Light sado-masochism in the art class failed to arouse the people of Bonnybridge beyond the level of casual, whispered confidences, just as the heavy-duty sadism of Smith was a matter of complete indifference. In late 1950s Scotland, ordinary life could go on in the streets of a small town without any recognition that behind the doors of the new school on the periphery, ostensibly a monument to educational progress and investment, children were not being taught, were not being loved and were not being cared for; children were being brutalised with the tacit approval of an enlightened state.

One day I stopped going. I don't remember it as a conscious decision. I simply woke up one morning and didn't go. Instead I went to an unobtrusive bus stop on the edge of the village and boarded a bus for Glasgow in my school uniform. The driver took my fare, asked no questions, and I went all the way to Buchanan Street bus station, a dark, dreary terminus, and from there wandered the streets of the city. I didn't eat; I had used part of my school lunch money on the fare and worked out that, if I repeated this exercise five days a week, I would have just enough for the bus and nothing left for anything else. I was truanting on a tight budget.

I discovered how easy it was for a 12-year-old boy in a big city to become invisible. No-one so much as glanced at me. I merged into the crowd in Sauchiehall Street, taking shelter from the rain in shop doorways, and still no-one expressed any interest in me. I watched with envy people having meals in cafes. I gazed at the tall Victorian buildings with their important-sounding enterprises advertised on ornate windows, and studied the nameplates at the entrance to offices, wondering what a notary might do for a living. I didn't dare go into department stores for fear of arousing suspicion, but observed with fascination the giant presses of the *Daily Record*, visible from Hope Street, which would soon be rolling with the first edition of its evening paper. I wandered into Central Station and looked at the train times for places I'd never heard of. Paisley Gilmour Street. Ardrossan Harbour. People hurrying. People with a purpose. In this throng only I was not hurrying; only I had no purpose. I was merely passing the time, avoiding the wrath of Miss Smith, that was my only purpose. Was I being missed back at Denny High? The thought never crossed my mind. My existence was wholly temporary and driven by expediency.

I returned to the house in the early afternoon – taking care to avoid my mother who usually came home for lunch – and waited.

'Good day at school?'

'Yes, not bad.'

The same ritual the next day, and the next, and the next, and still my parents never suspected, and still it seemed no-one at the school had noticed my absence. It went on for – how long? I'm not sure. Many weeks, certainly. Long enough for the chill of autumn to give way to the slush of winter. By then I was bolder, going as often to Falkirk as to Glasgow, exposing myself to the greater risk of being spotted in a town only a few miles from Bonnybridge, where my mother went Saturday shopping and both my parents knew people. But still no-one asked what I was doing on a school day, sporting the uniform of Denny High School (for some reason I believed in keeping up appearances) in the streets of Falkirk; not even in the cafes where I had a mid-morning cup of tea, now being able to afford one because the fare from Bonnybridge to Falkirk was so much cheaper.

One snowy morning in February 1958, I looked with disbelief at the billboard of a newsagents in Falkirk: almost the entire Manchester United football team, the 'Busby Babes', had been wiped out in the Munich air disaster. It was one of the few moments when I allowed myself to feel any emotion. For most of the time, I was without feeling; cauterised. I concentrated on the daily strategy for survival, which meant, above every other consideration, staying invisible.

Eventually, a letter arrived from the school drawing my parents' attention to my prolonged absence and requesting a meeting. My parents were understandably shocked. I crumbled – I was barely coherent – and my mother phoned our GP, Dr Fowler, who advised that I should be put to bed to await his arrival. He checked me out for physical symptoms – there were none – and asked a few questions about my state of mind and if anything had been upsetting me at school. I said that school had been getting me down, but was no more specific. I was too terrified to grass on Smith.

After a few days, my mother accompanied me to a meeting with the headmaster. I remember nothing of what was said by either party, but at the end of it I was told that I would be returning to class. I assumed he meant a lower class, I guessed C, where I could catch up on lost work at a gentler pace. But no: I was to go straight back to the pressure cooker of the A class.

My mother left, and the headmaster escorted me back in the middle of a period. After a few words with the subject teacher, he too left and the teacher pointed meaningfully to the one empty seat, the one so long vacated. The room fell silent as I resumed my place. None of my peers acknowledged me. For what was left of the period, the teacher ignored me. I went on being shunned during the breaks. I seemed to have acquired the status of pariah.

With intense dread, I anticipated the double period of mathematics. I needn't have worried. Smith too ignored me (as did Riach; as did all the others). For weeks I had been invisible on the streets of Glasgow and Falkirk; now I was invisible in the classrooms of Denny High School. An instruction must have gone out that the wretched boy was trouble and should be left severely alone. I barely listened to the lessons: I couldn't follow most of them, I had missed too much, there seemed little point. Instead I detached myself mentally, and no-one bothered me. But it did seem – or was it my imagination? – that Smith was belting less often and less ferociously. Had there been some change of policy?

Foolishly I pretended to my parents that I was 'getting back to normal' and 'catching up'. There was no suggestion that, if I were to have any chance of 'catching up', I would need a crash course in all my subjects, after-hours tuition, home visits. Nor did there appear to be any attempt by the school to keep in touch with my parents or to supervise any small progress I might be making (not that I was making any). It made the theft of the report card all the easier.

Reports began to appear in the local newspapers that all was not well at Denny High; it emerged that the Stirlingshire education authority had instigated a formal inquiry into its management. The word 'anarchy' was used to describe the atmosphere in the school. The report of the inquiry was never published (so far as I know), but as a result of it the headmaster was dismissed. The arch-sadist Smith survived the investigation, but as a diminished figure; no doubt she had received some sort of warning.

I don't know how much my own experience impacted on any of this. I suspect the situation was rumbled by decent members of the staff, of whom there were a few. I now had this much in common with Smith: we had both been marginalised. But I had formed a plan to get my own back on Denny High School, which had deprived me of an education (as I saw it, anyway) and ruined any prospect I might have had of going to university.

One of the newspapers in the house at the weekend was Beaverbook's *Sunday Express*, then a power in the land. One Sunday I noticed with the greatest excitement that it was launching a short-story competition for schoolchildren all over the UK. Aspiring writers were given a number of fictional intros and invited to complete the story in 500 words. I chose to write about an air crash (prophetic, as in later life I was involved in one). I sent off my entry and waited.

There was no advance notification of the results to the award-winners, so I had the satisfaction of learning from the newspaper that, from thousands of submissions, I was runner-up in my age category. I won enough money (£100) to buy a brand-new set of John Letters golf clubs.

I went to school on Monday with no expectation that anyone at Denny would be aware of the *Sunday Express* competition or my successful part in it. But at morning assembly, there was really only one item on the agenda: the great honour visited on the school by my triumphant debut in the literary world. I was invited to rise and receive the acclamation of the school. From pariah to local hero – it was bewildering.

An English teacher, a recognisable human being, Miss Dunn (Elizabeth, as I came to know her when years later I opened her husband's church fete), offered to come to the house and give me tuition in the forlorn hope that I might be able to pass in English if nothing else. On her first visit, the TV was on in the living room, where the tuition was to take place. I expected my parents to turn it off. They didn't. I blushed with embarrassment. Despite Miss Dunn's best efforts, I didn't pass in English. I didn't pass in a single subject. Yet I did receive a 'junior leaving certificate', which my mother retained, possibly in the mistaken assumption that it was of some sentimental value. After my mother died, Linda found it among her things and returned it to me. One glance at my junior leaving certificate was enough to confirm that it was a meaningless piece of parchment in fancy lettering, basically a formal acknowledgement that I had attended school. I hadn't even done that with any consistency. I wasn't entitled to the junior leaving certificate. When it came in the post, I should have destroyed it.

On my last day at Denny High – the school broke up early at end of term – I left without saying goodbye to anybody and walked the familiar way home, a couple of miles through woodland. The woodland has gone, having got in the way of the new dual carriageway between Glasgow and Stirling. The school building has gone too. New in 1957, it was demolished after barely half a century, though as I'll report presently, not without one last visit from me.

Before I left the old, rural, pre-dual carriageway road, before Denny High disappeared from sight, before I entered the woodland, I looked back at the school and stood there transfixed for several minutes. I thought that nothing that happened to me in my life could ever make me so miserable as Denny High School. I was to be proved correct. Nothing ever came close.

Smith continued to haunt me. She would appear as a monstrous figure in nightmares. For a long time, I felt she might be just around the next corner. The fear was visceral. Occasionally I had an almost irresistible urge to find out where she lived and confront her. Even as I prepare to die, she is the one human being I cannot find it in my heart to forgive.

The residual problem was a sense of personal guilt. That too haunted me for years. How come I, apparently alone of the hundreds of boys who attended Denny High School, how come I couldn't hack it when everybody else could? What was so special – so uniquely sensitive – about me that I couldn't put up with Smith for a few hours a week, take the sting of her tawse and the bite of her tongue, and then forget about her? How did this malevolent woman so get under my skin that she altered the course of my life, making me an altogether darker personality? I go on searching, but I receive no answers. Except that the problem was not Smith. It was essentially me.

A coda. A long time ago, when I was a telly celeb, the headteacher – no more headmasters – of Denny High School invited me to dish out the prizes at the end of term.

It was too intriguing a proposition to pass up. I looked out to a gratifying spectacle: hundreds of pupils with bright, smiling faces. They even had a school orchestra. I began my speech with a reference to ex-dux Fred, joking – though it was no joke – that they'd invited the wrong Roy. It all went well. And, yes, the place did seem smaller and less intimidating than it had in 1957.

1pm. Dr Gillen comes for a chat and stays for almost an hour. He says he is glad to see me looking brighter, but we don't talk much about me. We talk about the need for a greater spirit of co-operation between artists and scientists, about his love of literature and the theatre, about the calamity of Brexit and how the idealistic young feel cheated by it, about the sources of inspiration of the professional life (curiosity, endless curiosity about the day ahead) and about the need for kindness in hospital. He felt that keenly when he was in hospital himself not long ago. I could only murmur agreement. It is a shame I am about to die. I sense a kindred spirit. We might have become friends.

3pm. Visit from a consultant in palliative care. We talk round the subject of 'where I am now' and 'what I need now', and how where I am and what I need has changed since the last time she saw me, I remember not when. I feel a bit uneasy in her company and perhaps she in mine. She asks me what I'm writing and I try to explain, boasting that I've written almost 20,000 words since last weekend. She says I must be an extremely good typist. True enough, I suppose.

4.15pm. No visitors this afternoon. A new experience. Speak to M on the phone. Steven enters bearing pillows. He is suffering from a surfeit of pillows and wonders if

I'd like one. Natch. He props it behind my head, giving me more support. He's wondering who else will take one.

Muffled voices from reception. After a stormy morning, it looks slightly calmer out there, but the forecast for the weekend is poor. It is of no concern to me. I appreciate my little patch of sky, and monitor it regularly for subtle changes in colour and tone.

Dinner soon. It does come round. After the year I've had, eating a constant source of anxiety, I no longer enjoy food. I pick at it, always mindful of the possible consequences. Each mealtime a minefield to be negotiated. I negotiate this one, but relief when it's over and there is no acid reflux to speak of. Yet.

6pm. Visit from Fiona. She relates an amusing story about Islay's journey to work this morning. Islay felt something on her shoulder and swatted it away. Whatever it was landed on someone further up the bus, who also got rid of it pronto. It turned out to be a spider. The third recipient caught it on a bit of paper and calmly deposited it in her handbag, informing her bemused fellow passengers that she was concerned for the creature's well-being and would ensure, when she left the bus, that it was deposited in a suitably safe environment. Islay is full of these stories from the No. 4, but insect welfare is a new one.

Christina, at the end of a 12-hour stint, puts her head round the door to say she's off for a few days and looking forward to a night at the Grand Central Hotel in Glasgow with her boyfriend. Surprise surprise, they intend to spend a little time in the champagne bar. Christina and Fiona exchange fashion notes on some royal wedding today, of which I was blissfully unaware. And, before he leaves for the weekend, Steven joins us. The pillow problem is no nearer a solution. He thought he'd dump some in an empty side-room, but someone had got there first. When he opened the door he almost collapsed under the weight of pillows.

Fiona brings the latest mail from the office, including, from Maggie Mellon, a little book of poems edited by Jackie Kay on the theme of kindness. Kindness has become the word of the day. The book, published in memory of a boy who took his own life, includes a beautiful memoir by his mother, Lucy Alexander. It's a special gift.

I'd hoped for the lost 3,000 words to be safely installed on the laptop tonight, but a further small technical hitch has occurred and I shall have to wait a few more days. Fiona assures me that the 3,000 words are safe; she has seen the 3,000 words; she can practically recite the 3,000 words. All right. I believe it.

8pm. It's Stacey on duty tonight. I've been unwired now for nine hours – the longest off a machine since I arrived – so curious, and more than a little concerned, to see the effect on BP. 'It's actually better than it was,' reports Stacey. 'In fact it's the best I've seen it.' A rare morsel of good news. Always a downside, though: my temperature is up slightly for no obvious reason.

9.40pm. Linda texts to offer to put together a CD of my favourite music. Islay produced one a week or so ago, very good it was too, but I couldn't bear to listen for long; too evocative of mood, place, etc. Best to avoid the evocative; it's bad for the health. I do wish I could be more grown-up about this. I'm denying myself access to news (no hardship, as I've made clear before), books, films and music, because, as already observed, they all have the capacity to cause grief or upset by the power of association. Instead I write. I do nothing but write, obsessively, checking the word count as I go along. These words are all I have left. They are my refuge. They are life-sustaining. Without them I die. I die anyway. But these words, which look so fresh and appealing, prove to me that, in the face of death, I can still string a few sentences together, which is really all I've ever wanted to do.

I text sis back and say thanks, I'll think about it.

10.30pm. Stacey brings the meds. I don't know if it's worth bothering with the sleeping pill; although relatively strong, it is not proving to be all that effective. There is no point in saying that I dread the small hours. You know that already. I am sorry about the repetitions. But if I repeat something often enough, you can take it it's true.

Stacey says there's no need for a BP check tonight. I'm okay. I'm fine.

1am. Still awake, restless, bit of indigestion, fearful it's something worse, barely able to comprehend the implications of the position I'm in. This room, can it be true I'll never leave it alive? This bed, is it really my death bed? That ticking clock with the wrong date, could it be the last thing I hear? Do I really leave the world facing two signs that say TOILET? I could never have anticipated any of this three weeks ago, ill as I felt. I could never have imagined this room, the corridor outside it, those blue plastic chairs with the spare pyjamas ready for tomorrow (or later in the night if I miss target), the pee bottles, the sick bags, the endless supplies of Lucozade, my name tag and date of birth forever attached to my wrist, the laxatives, the commode, the big red chair in the corner – I don't think I've mentioned the big red chair before – it's the one for my special guests. I call it the Val Doonican chair.

But it could be worse. Of course. Fiona reminded me last night that I might have died of a sudden heart attack, or as the result of a car crash, in which case there would have been no opportunity for fond farewells. Unusually, I have also been able to read my own obituaries, I suppose pre-obits would be a better way of describing them, which is a privilege afforded to few. But the authorised version – the one I took the precaution of writing myself, as dispassionately as possible, proverbial warts and all – won't be released until I've gone. I've asked Islay to post it on the *Scottish Review* home page, and interested parties can make what they like of it. The dates are approximately correct. I stand by the dates. There's only one missing, the date I can't help Islay with.

A private funeral. There is a piece of wild land on the edge of the village, far end of the cemetery, which is reserved for woodland burials. I liked the look of it when I checked it out not that long ago. I remember writer and friend Katie Grant telling me she knew exactly where she'd be buried (family plot in deepest Lancs; her lineage makes the Windsors look like upstarts); I sensed that knowing was a source of comfort. I don't feel that strongly about it, but a woodland burial does sound nice. I'm not sure I'd want to be incinerated, and the crematorium – 'the crem' to borrow Barbara's matey abbreviation – has never appealed. Soulless place, sickly organ music, a production line of death, 20 minutes and you're off, next please.

But do I really care? What does it matter? What does any of it matter?

2am. Still awake, agitated, so take the pill.

＊

Saturday 13 October

FIVE HOURS' UNBROKEN sleep – not bad. Ping of a text message wakes me up. Disorientated; promptly mislay the phone. Wait for the next ping in order to locate it. How did people manage in hospital when there was no access to mobile phones? Their introduction is surely the most helpful innovation for patients, a source of comfort as well as essential information. I know I'd be bereft without mine.

Alison, particularly friendly nurse I haven't seen for a few days because she's been on a city break to Milan, says she'll be looking after me all weekend. Good. She's up to speed about my difficulties and aware I won't be leaving. 'You're a keeper,' she adds brightly. Ironical mention of Christmas dinner. You can only laugh, which I do.

So I'm a keeper. I hadn't heard that one before.

The weekend cleaner not the happiest bunny. Somewhat grim, unresponsive to my feeble attempts to engage her, bangs clumsily about the room with her mop, goes. Okay. Be like that. See if I care.

Leaden sky. This is the first morning I've heard the rain. M says she's not going out, except to the village shop for the paper.

I'm missing my pal Steven. It's almost half eleven and he'd have been here long before now with the offer of a wash and a shave. Still unwired, I'd have a go at washing myself, but I need a towel and I don't like bothering them. Last thing I want is to acquire a reputation as one of the ward's constant bleepers. They are a menace. A man in an adjoining side-room, if he doesn't receive an immediate response, starts shouting repeatedly, 'Help! Help me, nurse! Help!' in a cry so desperate that at first I assumed he was about to breathe his last. He's been sussed. Trouble is, when he really is in trouble, no-one will know the difference.

Nice young girl, back on duty after three weeks off sick with a painful inner ear infection, has read my mind and brought a towel unasked. Ridiculous: I now have to mentally prepare myself to walk a few feet to the sink close to the bed. I'll try it and let you know how I get on.

Well, I managed: just. Was afraid of dizziness, falling, making an arse of myself. Didn't happen. So some improvement on earlier in the week. Just incredibly weak. Quick wash, back to bed. Maybe I'll have a sitting-down shower one of those days, you never know.

Saturday is the only day I miss a Wi-Fi connection. I still have a passing interest in football, and used to enjoy the half-hour at home on Saturday afternoon seeing the results coming in from such outposts as Exeter, Halifax, Ayr and Cowdenbeath. I never had much time for the big boys, and was pleased when someone noted in a book that I had an arcane fascination with no-hope lower league teams. East Stirlingshire, my first love, have sunk so low that they're reduced to the clapped-out stiffs of the Lowland League among such giants of the game as Hawick Royal Albert. But I haven't quite given up on them; or hadn't till I landed here without a Wi-Fi connection. Fiona did say David, our office neighbour, might find a way of fixing me up with one.

After last night's good news, BP down again. Alison exhorts me to drink as much as possible and she will check again in the afternoon. Pear and banana for lunch with, I hope, watermelon to follow when Barbara, my visitor from Fife (via Waitrose) gets here.

Watermelon delicious.

Nadia, bearing the dinner menu, says she is 'crabbit'. Scottish word signifying annoyed or fed up, often without a specific reason. This seems to be the case with Nadia. She turned up for work feeling crabbit and expects to be crabbit for the rest of the day. By the way, this smartarse laptop's dictionary has just tried to change crabbit to rabbit, which means that Nadia has turned up for work feeling rabbit.

9pm. Thinking about my two previous engagements with mortality before this final fixture of the season. When I was a young reporter with the BBC, I took part in an air rally organised by *Nationwide*, not the building society but a silly teatime telly programme which specialised in stunts and oddities of various kinds. A couple of old geezers from the Dundee flying club, with me as their tame gofer, set off in brilliant sunshine from Glasgow Airport representing our 'region' (Scotland, wouldn't you know) in competition with teams from the BBC's other 'regions', all of us headed for the finishing line at the Battle of Britain airfield at Biggin Hill. By the time our Piper Cherokee reached Kent, the sun was no longer shining and we were enveloped in a swirling, well-nigh impenetrable fog. Strange that the rally went ahead at all, as the pea-souper had been forecast by the Met Office. The Air Accidents Investigation Branch also thought it strange and heavily criticised the BBC for its irresponsibility. I could and should have taken my employer to the cleaners, but it never occurred to me.

Fortunately, only one aircraft was wrecked in the chaos over Biggin Hill – ours. We'd run out of fuel on the approach despite the navigator's confident assurance, at dinner in Glasgow the previous night, that our pilot was an RAF veteran who wouldn't take unnecessary risks. I don't know whether not having enough fuel in the engine qualified as a necessary risk, but it resulted in us having to overshoot the runway and head for the nearest field, where we nose-dived into a tree. Remarkably, all three on board clambered out with barely a scratch and, completing the absurdity of the occasion, the survivors were promptly ushered to an awards ceremony at which Scotland (the only region minus an aircraft) was declared the winner. I'd never met my fellow regional presenters, and was particularly unimpressed by the best-known of them, Stuart Hall, an odious, jumped-up chancer, who later went to prison for sex offences.

I was then driven into central London for the sleeper back to Scotland; it was only when I was safely on the train that I noticed I was mud-encased up to my knees. No-one had thought to have us medically examined. The negligence was staggering.

I only tell you this tedious little tale from my past because of its relevance to the over-arching theme of this book. Was I frightened by the prospect of my imminent and possibly messy death? I had several minutes to think about it as our captain relayed his mayday messages to Biggin Hill control. But I didn't experience anything resembling fear. I stayed calm, resigned to my fate, and as we came ever closer to our destination – the tree – I continued to stay calm. So what was that about?

My second near-death experience, 20 years later, was largely my own fault. Cursed with varicose veins, I'd allowed a clot on my left knee to grow to the size of a golf ball. The young GP in Girvan took one look at it and referred me to A and E at Ayr Hospital, where I was admitted at once and told to lie flat on my back for a spell of complete bed-rest. According to the specialist in clots the size of golf balls, nothing less than a week would do it. I was discharged with the clot looking no better, and a couple of nights later part of it chipped off and travelled to the lung. Back at the hospital I was told it was a pulmonary embolism. Did I remain calm on that occasion? I did not. I was panicking like mad. Near-fatal air accidents I could cope with in the course of a day's work, but clots the size of golf balls tended to freak me out. During my long recovery at home, I began to be curious about the week of complete bed-rest I'd been prescribed and sought a second opinion. The consultant who came to the house said that if I had been told to exercise vigorously and regularly, instead of being horizontally confined for a week, the clot would have dispersed naturally. That did seem quite a plausible theory.

You will have observed one essential difference between my first two brushes with death and the latest: there is no way out of this one. But there is a second difference of mild interest: the duration of each crisis. If the pulmonary embolism had killed me, it would have done so without undue delay. Similarly, if the Piper Cherokee hadn't run out of fuel but had instead burst into flames on impact, reducing the young reporter and his mates to charred corpses, our terminal agony would have been over quickly. It is the duration of the present crisis that gives it a distinctive quality. I don't know how long I will go on living – and I have no present intention of asking for an estimate – but I have already had time to write 22,000 words of a book, approve and sign employment contracts for colleagues, arrange for a literary executor to be appointed, write a farewell editorial for the *Scottish Review*, have regular meetings with close friends and family, speak to others on the phone, and attend to arrangements for my funeral. The fact that all of these activities, which make each day an active one, happen to have a single theme – my impending death – gives the experience an extraordinary unreality. I am as busy as ever, in some respects busier, yet I am a dead man walking. Or, rather, not walking. Much.

Sunday 14 October

TOOK THE PILL at 10.30pm last night, could feel myself drifting off, soon asleep. When I next looked at the clock it was 6.30am. Pulled the sheets over my head and snoozed for another hour.

Alison says she watched 'shite TV' last night. 'So that would be either *Strictly* or the *X Factor*,' I suggest. '*X Factor*,' she clarifies, 'although I'm not keen on Robbie Williams and his wife.' We agree that there's something to be said for shite TV on a Saturday night, especially if, like Alison, you've just come off a long, arduous shift in an NHS ward.

Sunday is a bit different in here. You never see a consultant and rarely a doctor (which is also true of Saturday) and there is no delivery of newspapers. At one time, no doubt, chaplains or the parish clergy would have been patrolling the wards quoting scripture, taking confessions and promoting the interests of the better life to come, but I haven't seen a single dog-collar since I arrived. It's a relief. If I want to have a chat with God, I hope I'm able to call him direct without the intercession of the holy chaps and chapesses, even if the call does go straight to voicemail.

Before I left my childhood home, I was a faithful attender at Bonnybridge Parish Church. I preferred the evening service (6.30) because there were no more than a couple of dozen in the pews, allowing the bright young minister, Tom Scott, son of a former moderator of the Kirk's General Assembly, to deliver the sort of high-end, intellectually challenging sermon that appealed to me. I still wasn't sure that I truly 'believed': the leap of faith, or the leap into faith, eluded me. But I did attempt to get through to God – through the formal mechanism they called prayer – during Tom's thoughtful services, with no serious expectation that there was anyone listening. I also sang the hymns, most of them execrable, and endured with a mixture of boredom and revulsion the obligatory reading from the Old Testament. I was not in favour of burning books, but I would have been tempted to burn the Old Testament, a malignant inspiration for many of the world's crackpot ideas. The New was beautifully written, though as per usual the journalists who pulled it together couldn't agree on some fairly basic stuff, and I was duly seduced by the story of the Resurrection, a piece of pure poetry, and by the attractive precepts of love and forgiveness.

All my life I enjoyed listening to religious thinkers: Tom Scott, Frank Martin (minister at Pitlochry, whose church, later converted into apartments, stood opposite the Festival Theatre, later converted into a curling rink), and at the BBC a variety of stimulating characters. I was particularly close to Ian Mackenzie (head of religious broadcasting) and Donald Macdonald (a brilliant maverick from North

Kenneth with parents Esther and Richard.

The family holiday photograph referred to in the 6 October entry.

The Roy family on holiday, now complete with Linda.

Kenneth (centre with arms folded) surrounded by Linda and cousins.

Kenneth and Linda c. 1960.

Family Christmas in Maybole Castle. Kenneth, Margaret, Stephen and Christopher (standing). Kenneth's mother, Esther, is on the left.

With Jimmy Reid. The honour which meant more to Kenneth than any other in his life was the invitation by the Reid family to conduct Jimmy's private funeral service.

With Magnus Magnusson, first patron of the Institute of Contemporary Scotland on the evening of its launch.

'Ordinary days' for Kenneth at his desk in the office at Prestwick Airport. They were something to be cherished and never taken for granted.

Kenneth in action chairing an event at the Young Programme – his 'pride and joy' – a Young England and Wales Programme in Lancaster.

With Amanda Williams (trustee, left) and Sheetal Ramesh Shah (former delegate, middle) at a Young Programme end of year occasion in North Queensferry.

With Islay McLeod (middle) on the occasion of her 10th anniversary of working with the charities founded by Kenneth. Barbara Millar is on the right (and supplied the cake!). The print on the wall is a plan of Inveramsay railway station.

In the spring sunshine at the Young England and Wales Programme in Lancaster in 2018 with Islay McLeod (left) and Fiona MacDonald (right).

Preparing adjudication notes at a Young Programme event in Lancaster, typically with coffee and shortbread at hand.

Kenneth's memorial service took place on 14 March 2019 in this magnificent room in Glasgow City Chambers (thanks to the generosity of Glasgow City Council). Young Programme 'young leaders' Sarah Tranter (left), Elliot Boakes (third from left) and Alexey Underwood (right), and Young Programme trustee Junior Deslandes (second from left) were ushers.

Uist, converted to Christianity by Billy Graham – which sounds preferable to being converted into apartments or a curling rink, though some will disagree). I once spent an engrossing afternoon in the eyrie-cum-study of the leading Scottish theologian of his day, Professor Tom Torrance, and asked him if God and Jesus were one and the same: the answer seemed to be yes. And I enjoyed the gentle company of the St Andrews theologian, Professor James Whyte, who brilliantly deconstructed for me Margaret Thatcher's bizarre interpretation of St Paul's words: 'If a man will not work, he shall not eat'. In other words, I had privileged access to the best contemporary thinking on religious belief and spirituality. But in the end it made no difference: I remained sceptical. Perhaps it was the journalist in me. Scepticism bred in the bone.

Late in life, the deep-thinking Scottish actor/comedian Rikki Fulton, with his wife Kate Matheson, began attending their local parish church in Glasgow. He told me, during a long conversation about God, that he too still hadn't made the leap. He couldn't, quite. 'But I love the questions. Oh, the questions…' He smiled and I smiled with him, in instinctive agreement. The questions. We loved the questions.

After years of non-attendance, I returned to church occasionally when we went to live in the castle at Maybole. The incumbent was a dry old stick, George Anderson, very much on the theological right, but I didn't mind dry old sticks in the pulpit. The ones I minded were the new breed of manic 'happy clappies' (so called), who wanted us to embrace each other, sing loud hallelujahs, and generally rejoice. One Christmas, at Girvan, where we'd gone to live after we couldn't afford the castle at Maybole any more, they brought drums and bagpipes into the kirk. I didn't go back; I don't think I've ever been back.

I have an aversion to being obliged to embrace the person sitting next to me, even in Christian fellowship. I wouldn't mind doing it voluntarily with a consenting adult, but not to order as part of some formal love-in. The communal singing of modern feel-good ditties, full of soppy sentiments, is likewise repellent. The sermons, if they are still called sermons, amount to no more than simplistic slogans. And now, I gather, there is a phenomenon known as the 'messy church', where anything goes, especially when badly behaved children are being indulged.

The cause of Christianity in Scotland has not been enhanced by the pomposity, bad faith and cruelty of many of its more prominent adherents. I must sadly record that some of the nastiest people I encountered as a journalist and broadcaster were ministers of the Church of Scotland. If I don't feel as strongly about the other denominations, perhaps it is only because I came into contact with them less.

Two of the men I mentioned earlier – Ian Mackenzie and Donald Macdonald – were both destroyed – I don't use the word lightly – by the hierarchy of their own church. I'll say a little about each because their experiences have inevitably coloured my judgement of God's ambassadors on earth.

Ian Mackenzie came to the BBC in Scotland via the parish ministry in Peterhead and a creative interlude as a television producer in London. He started in the Scottish job determined to challenge the conventional notions of 'religious' television – in particular the Church of Scotland's arrogant assumption that it had an entitlement to airtime for the transmission of church services that hardly anyone watched. The entitlement extended to coverage of the annual General Assembly, which was expected to be generous and generally benevolent in tone, and which, again, hardly anyone watched. For years, the Kirk's demands, formally articulated through such channels as the BBC's 'religious advisory committee' and the Broadcasting Council for Scotland, were satisfied more or less without dissent. BBC Scotland decided it would rather show programmes that hardly anyone watched than pick a quarrel with so powerful an institution as the Church of Scotland. But then along came Mackenzie.

I was centrally involved in both his initial innovations. He hired me as presenter of a series called *Eighth Day*, transmitted live early on Sunday evening, which attempted to give the news of the week a deeper dimension, looking at stories from an ethical or spiritual standpoint. Ian's approach to this demanding brief was blithely extempore. We didn't meet until lunchtime on Sunday, which made the pace of preparation as hectic as any bog-standard news programme. Ian's own essay of the week, cobbled together in the BBC canteen, made an elegant counterpoint to the polemic of Donald Macdonald, the other regular talking head. I was left to conduct the studio interviews, often arranged at the shortest notice with public figures falling over themselves to appear on the box (in broadcasting, human vanity tends to overcome any small logistical difficulties such as walking over hot coals to get to the studio). It was the strangest programme, yet somehow it worked. But it didn't return for a second series. It was Ian's opening salvo directed at the Church of Scotland; the first sign that he intended to do things his way.

If the Kirk's collective nose was beginning to twitch by the last episode of the irreverent *Eighth Day*, it was positively bristling when Ian launched *The Yes, No, Don't Know Show*, a 45-minute audience debate on such questions as 'Is God dead?'. The audience voted yes, no or don't know at the start. I then moved in among them eliciting opinions and provoking argument, and there was a second vote at the end. It was a format that later became familiar, wearily so, but at the time (mid-1970s) it was quite new and daring. The programme often ascended into near-anarchy, which I saw no reason to discourage as the audience, random members of the public, threw verbal darts at each other. It made for lively, thought-provoking late night television, and I was proud of it. The ratings soared – no product of BBC Scotland's religious department had ever achieved a higher audience – and a second series was commissioned, moving the programme out of the Glasgow studio into community halls in various parts of the country. But the Church of Scotland hated it. Ian and his boss, Alastair Hetherington, the Scottish controller, were summoned to various meetings in Edinburgh and brusquely informed that the series lacked structure and rigour and that it was only loosely 'religious'. It certainly bore little obvious resemblance to the flagship of BBC religious TV, *Songs of Praise*.

The pressure on Ian was intense, especially when his predecessor in the job turned on him, and the attacks were both venomous and deeply personal. I was protected from most of the flak, but I couldn't help being generally aware that my own professionalism was being called into question by anonymous bureaucrats who felt no moral obligation to confront me openly. Ian rode the storm, up to a point, but there were days when he looked grey and broken. One day, he pointed to a letter on his desk in his own handwriting.

'It's my resignation,' he said. 'I'm not going to hand it in immediately, but it's there if I need it.' The letter stayed on his desk for several years, until a massive heart attack nearly killed him and he was forced into early retirement. He made the most of that retirement, writing, broadcasting and preaching, and I was pleased to commission and publish his autobiography, *I Was Invited*. But the reforming zeal had gone. The Kirk had seen to that.

The ordeal of Donald Macdonald was more painful still. He was a hugely popular and inspirational parish minister in the working-class district of Glasgow Partick, as I was able to observe for myself when he invited me to open some function or other. In addition to the day job, he found time to write and broadcast with enviable fluency and force. He described himself as a Christian Marxist (perhaps he was the last of that breed), although theologically he was a conservative: he was a real mixed-up kid. He made a mistake in leaving the parish ministry to join the BBC full-time; he was unhappy at the BBC and took ever more heavily to the bottle.

Donald lost his licence to preach in circumstances that I forget. He was thus cut adrift. Towards the end, he applied to the Kirk (through its Glasgow Presbytery) for the restoration of that licence, not because he had any intention of reapplying for the parish ministry – it was too late for that – but because he wished to be able to conduct funerals and weddings. He was ill (as it turned out he was dying). It didn't seem a lot to ask considering his long service to the Church of Scotland. When the application was refused, he turned to me for help. Would I say a few words on his behalf in my weekly column in *Scotland on*

Sunday? I was more than happy to oblige; I wrote more than one column about the inhumanity of a church turning its back on one of its own, a soul palpably in distress. A fat lot of good it did. The licence was not restored, and Donald died in his early 50s, disgracefully abandoned by his fellow Christians in his hour of need.

The dreadful treatment of Ian Mackenzie and Donald Macdonald, two of the brightest people I ever knew, soured me towards the Church of Scotland, and I am glad that its influence has waned, that it is running out of money and manpower, and that the media no longer take it that seriously. I doubt that it deserves to survive. I discovered that there was something rotten at its core. Its problem – a rather serious one – was a want of Christian charity.

Hope God is nicer than so many of his servants.

8.45pm. Before she left for the night, Alison showed me a photo of the new love of her life, her pup Lola, a Jack Russell.

I started to feel ever so slightly queasy an hour ago and the night nurse has given me an anti-sickness pill. Do hope I'm not facing a bad night.

Monday 15 October

7.15pm. A bad night? The worst. The queasiness didn't lift, and by 4am I was experiencing a weird clamminess (though my temperature was normal), a sign that my bloods were dangerously low. I called the nurse, who called the ANP, who called the night doctor, and soon the room was full of medics and machinery.

I got through the rest of the night somehow, having slept not a wink, and by the morning felt utterly dreadful and was convinced that this day would be my last. Sent the usual dire texts. An auxiliary came to change my bed and asked me to move on to the Val Doonican chair. As soon as I did, I felt dizzy and threw up. It was another instalment of blackened blood from the stomach.

Dr Gillen comes to see me. 'I can't leave you for a minute,' he jokes. He begins by saying that what had happened didn't mean it's the end, although I form the unarticulated impression that it is pretty close. He then outlines a procedure of his that might lessen the internal bleeding and give me some respite. He asks if I am up for it; it would mean another trip to endoscopy. 'I'm up for it,' I reply, 'but I'd have to go in my own bed. I'm now terrified of moving out of it.' He said that would be no problem.

'I'm glad I have you as my doctor,' I say.

'I'm glad I have you as my patient,' he says.

Without delay, I am wheeled down to endoscopy, still wired to my drip, and given a strong local anaesthetic. Feel nothing. They take me straight back to my room. I am drowsy for several hours and beyond exhausted. I am to get the result of the procedure tomorrow.

Tuesday 16 October

ALMOST A SURPRISE NOW to be in the land of the living by dawn. Dr Gillen confirms that the procedure, covering the tumour with some sort of powder, was a success. But he is realistic. Quick fix and all that.

Visit from the palliative care consultant. Update on latest grisly events, with which she has been acquainted. I'm full of praise (as ever) for the medical and nursing teams who enabled me to pull through. 'And do you want to go on being pulled through?' she asks softly. Shocking question. I can only mutter 'Yes'. She smiles and I am left to digest the thought.

After she's gone, Linda and David arrive. I am now thoroughly downcast, barely able to speak. 'And do you want to go on being pulled through?' are the only words in my head. What am I to take out of them?

Seek a meeting with Hazel, who gives me her understanding of what is going on. The vomiting incidents so far are what the medics describe as 'insults'. Insults they can handle. Insults are nasty, but non-life-threatening. But she fears, and maybe expects, a 'catastrophic' bleed that will see me off. When it happens, I will be made as comfortable as possible. Of course. She holds my hand tightly.

For the next couple of hours, in the company of my sister and brother-in-law, I say very little. They have brought wet wipes (aloe vera, soothing aroma), whose application sends me into an untroubled sleep for maybe 20 minutes. This laptop's dictionary is all too prescient about my condition: it has just changed 'soothing aroma' to 'soothing coma'.

My niece Jenny is expecting a baby in mid-November. Death and life in the family. The old, old cycle. She and Pete have a son, Marley, aged four, who says he is writing a book. Linda shows me a photograph of the wee boy at his desk. 'Who does he remind you of?', Linda asks. I have to admit that he bears more than a passing resemblance to Gloomy Joe – without the gloom. I will die content knowing that Jenny and Pete, being thoroughly modern parents, will not inflict on their children the Roy curse of being instructed to be 'Be Somebody'. May all the children of Scotland be spared such a start in life.

Fiona, who comes in a bit later with Islay, reminds me that West Sound (local radio thing I started) came on air 37 years ago tonight. Unmoved by the news, which reminds me of too many characters I'd rather forget, except that it was how Fiona and I met, she a slip of lass not long out of university. By way of celebration, she smoked a menthol cigarette (Consulate). I've never seen her smoke since.

4pm. After nearly five hours of visitors, I'm on my own. The day of the ultimate question, 'And do you want to go on being pulled through?' Maybe she's right. Maybe I've suffered enough.

I'm noticing how my language is becoming steadily stripped back; such energy in the use of words as I had even a few days ago more or less gone. Now I merely record.

7pm. Visit from Fiona after work. 'Are you frightened?', she asks suddenly. 'No,' I reply honestly. Spare her the qualification: 'Only of the process.'

7.30pm. Hazel, on her way home, calls to say goodnight. 'Try to behave yourself,' she says. 'I know it's difficult.' Then Cheryl, who's working in another part of the ward. Such small acts of kindness assume a very much larger significance for people who are terminally ill.

Alison is night nurse: an exemplary mixture of compassion and practicality. Can't speak too highly of the backbone of this place: the nurses. I should have recorded that long ago.

11.30pm. I've just popped my first anti-anxiety pill. The

window blind rattles occasionally in the wind.
Midnight. Am I less anxious? Hard to say.

Wednesday 17 October

SLEEP A LOT TODAY. An unexpected visit – in fact over the course of the day three visits – from Dr Gillen. The second and third are social, but the first is to inform me that there is more to be done. My blood count is low, and he proposes to give me four transfusions today. He continues to be encouraged by the lack of spread to other vital organs. Sensing the possibility that I am admitting defeat, he adds that he would like to see me back at my laptop working on my writing. On one of his later visits, he reminds me that I am defined by writing, 'not by all this malarkey'. What a guy.

So maybe if I'm feeling up to it, I could do a piece of 'serious' writing tonight.

7.45pm. It occurs to me, for example, that I haven't said much about Bonnybridge other than in relation to my own family. A children's poet once made a careful study of a map of the British Isles for the prettiest place names and assembled them in a melodious arrangement. The medley consisted of just that and nothing more: the names themselves.

The poem only goes to show how deceptive place names can be. Bonnybridge, far from being some rural idyll, is a dark product of the industrial revolution, known locally – by which I mean in the smug neighbouring town of Falkirk, itself no oil painting – as 'Dirty Bonnybrig' or

'Dirty Wee Bonnybrig'. Yet with no apparent hint of irony we were expected to recite this outrageous ditty in the early years of primary school, the teacher always ready to rebuke any child who dared to snigger at the inclusion of Bonnybridge. It all had to be done with the straightest face.

This lie was the only thing we were ever taught about our native village throughout our primary education. Yet we could see the contrary evidence all too clearly for ourselves on our way to school. The Bonny Bridge passed over a burn of unspeakable filthiness, close to the premises of the taciturn local barber, the lanky Mr Hall, and the points of interest scenically were no more edifying than belching factory chimneys. The main products included household stoves ('the Esse') and bricks. (Children not doing well at school were warned by their fathers, including mine, that they would 'end up in the brickworks'; many did.) The only hotel – the Royal – was, like most establishments of that name, devoid of aesthetic pleasure or human comfort. The Public Hall, where my father produced his plays, smelled of old wood. The commercial hub of the village consisted of several branches of the Bonnybridge Co-operative Society, the windows groaning with every conceivable human need from a pork chop to a power drill. One day, before a special occasion of some kind, my mother marched me down to the clothing department and we surveyed a display of boys' smart wear. 'Trousers or kilt?' she demanded to know. 'Trousers,' I replied without hesitation. I never did wear a kilt.

For years we languished in a near-derelict block known as Caledonia Crescent on the banks of the Forth and Clyde canal, then still in daily use as a commercial waterway. My dog, the only one I ever had, drowned in it. I have occasionally been challenged to remember the poor dog's name, and I can't.

Life in Bonnybridge improved after the Second World War with the election of a Labour government and the creation of a huge council estate rising in steep tiers, each row identical to those before and after, all the way up to the Denny Road, the allocation of the houses largely in the gift of the local Labour councillors, Davie Mann and his son Alfie. Few dared to question the authority of the Mann family; they too (like the teachers, the clergy and the doctors) being beneficiaries of the universal compliance that distinguished the lives of working-class people who were expected to be grateful for what they'd got, and all too often were.

Although the councillors Mann were formally subject to democratic scrutiny at the elections to Stirlingshire County Council, Bonnybridge voted Labour automatically, local Tories being as rare as snakes in Ireland, which allowed the Mann family free rein for decades. The peasants, who were assessed on a strict points system before the precious tenancy was offered, received the most obvious gift of the socialist paradise: somewhere half-decent to live, a house which gave children the dignity of their own room and a garden to play in, front and back. I rather fancied myself as a meteorologist, and started measuring rainfall, a hobby impossible in the squalor of Caledonia Crescent.

We were among the first households in the village to have commercial television, and although the programmes were cheap imported rubbish (Roy Thomson's infamous 'permit to print money'), the ads introduced us to a seductive world of consumerism, in which gleaming new washing machines replaced the familiar drudgery. But there was a downside: my father predicted bleakly that, with the coming of commercial TV, there would soon be no audience for his productions in the Public Hall. He was right. The hall fell into disuse and was demolished, along with the local cinema, the Bug House, where my grandmother delighted in taking me to see lurid B-pictures. (There was not much respect for the classifications of the British Board of Film Censors at the Bug House.)

Yet our knowledge of the outside world was painfully circumscribed. I was startled one day to be told that we were all leaving the classroom for a couple of hours. We were led by our noses to the nearby green hut, the most basic community centre, and ordered to sit down in front of a black and white television set and watch events unfold 400 miles away in London, a city known only by name to any of us. Grainy images of the young queen and her husband processing majestically in a golden coach through crowded streets of cheering people meant nothing to us. After it was over we trooped back to our desks and resumed our studies, no more than mildly engaged by what we had just witnessed, if engaged at all.

Three years earlier, something of more direct interest had happened in Bonnybridge without any of the villagers knowing about it. It was while we were asleep. A party of idealistic young Scottish nationalists led by Ian Hamilton made a daring raid on Westminster Abbey on Christmas Day 1950 and removed the Stone of Destiny, over which monarchs had rested their bottoms during coronation ceremonies for more than 600 years. The raiders did even better: they managed to smuggle the stone back over the border to what they considered its rightful home. What to do with it there, particularly as half of Scotland was on the lookout for the perpetrators of this audacious coup? In the absence of any clear plan, it was decided to enlist the help of a renowned patriot, a man of unimpeachable credentials: John Rollo, employer of both my mother and my uncle. Under cover of darkness the precious object was taken by car to the St Andrew's Engineering Works where Rollo secreted it under the floorboards of my uncle George's office, and there it stayed for several weeks, unknown to uncle George or to my mother, who continued to type letters for her boss oblivious to the momentous significance of what was going on around – or rather under – her.

Although she was devoted to John Rollo, she was never attracted by his political creed, an independent Scotland. She and my father, and everyone they knew, voted Labour, not because they had any illusions about the Manns, but because voting Labour was the most practical route to the promised land. To the end of her life, my mother was singing the praises of Labour politicians, her last favourite Gordon Brown, a friend of the old folk who would never let the old folk down (in her judgement). But I don't remember politics being talked about much in the house when I was a boy, and certainly not nationalist politics. The SNP, if it rated a mention at all, was dismissed as a joke. (Within half a century, Bonnybridge was a nationalist stronghold and the local SNP councillor was planning to promote the village as a world tourist centre of extra-terrestrials, my mother's old house, Bonnyside, having been identified as a hotbed of nocturnal goings-on of an unexplained nature, allegedly alien in origin.)

It would have aided our understanding – it would have been genuinely educational – if we had known something of the history of our own community before the aliens improbably chose Bonnybridge as their regional headquarters: how the village came into being through the needs of heavy industry, abruptly transforming a small agrarian economy into a capitalist one. We would have learned the importance of migration – the brutal movement of people into our community to service the machine – and of transport – why the railway and the canal were so vital to the village's commercial prosperity – and we would have learned, too, why so much of the housing was so wretched and why, 100 years later, so much of it had not been replaced. In short, we would have known much more about our immediate forefathers, and the far from benevolent external forces that had shaped their lives, than we were ever taught at school. The conspiracy to keep generations of children in the dark – to deprive them of essential information – was not some aberration of the Stirlingshire education authority; it was official policy throughout the country and it was blatantly political. There was no more powerful weapon for quashing the reforming spirit than ignorance: what the child had never known the child could never question. Safer the date of an obscure English battle than a curious look round the next corner.

R. F. Mackenzie, whose work has inspired so much of what I have thought and done in my life, writes about this matter in much greater depth in his masterly *A Search for Scotland*. I can't recommend his book highly enough.

8.45pm. Leanne, night nurse, says she's heard I've finished the book. I explain that I thought I had, but that Dr G has persuaded me it's open-ended and should carry on as long as I do. Leanne believes such a book could be immensely helpful in letting fellow cancer sufferers know that they are not alone. She speaks from experience: her young husband was diagnosed five years ago and is still in remission.

Thursday 18 October

STEVEN IS BACK after a few days off, how I've missed him, and he offers to give me that sitting-down shower we've been talking about for ages. He settles me on the commode and guides me gently through to the bathroom and we're good to go. The joy of having one's hair washed and dried for the first time in weeks. A routine that one used to take for granted, think nothing of, now an event to be considered and negotiated. I no longer bemoan this crushing reversal of fortune, the all too swift descent into helplessness. 'Look at me,' I say to Steven. 'I'm standing and not falling.' This is how I assess my daily life now, marvelling at my ability to stay erect and relatively stable for a few seconds. Dr Gillen thought yesterday that I might yet get out into the hospital grounds. It sounds crazy, but then writing properly again, until he cajoled me into doing it, sounded crazy too.

I have discovered that it is best not to look at diaries or calendars, those reference points to times past and future. Before I left the office for the last time, I shredded my 2018 diary, the one Islay gave me at Christmas, and threw it in the bin along with all my diaries from previous years: I knew I had no further use for them. Time as I understood it ceased at that symbolic moment. I now maintain an alternative diary that I call overtime, which is all in the mind with no need to write anything down and no known closing date. It is a diary for the dying.

I've just remembered. I have no shoes. I have no memory of where I left them. And, beyond a few quid someone gave me to buy a paper in the morning, which I resolutely don't, I have no money either. What else don't I have? I'm not sure I have trousers, unless pyjama bottoms count. I don't have a jacket to my name. My wallet – it's somewhere else too, no doubt in safe hands – its loss would once have had me sweating, all those bank cards and bus passes and train tickets and god-awful VAT receipts. That doesn't bother me either. Here in overtime, the first thing to go is any interest whatever in possessions.

But small luxuries continue to be valued, although I wouldn't have regarded them as luxuries when I still kept a proper diary, got on the bus with Islay in the morning, climbed the stairs of Liberator House, watched the planes come and go, wrote editorials, planned trips, snoozed on the sofa in the afternoon, went home in the evening, did the crossword, watched some Welsh noir on the telly, etc. For example, I have developed an irresistible craving for the luxury of strong black builder's tea, with two sugars. In the middle of the night, when they were changing over the units of blood in the machine, I prevailed on Cheryl to make me a brew. She did so uncomplainingly because that's how Cheryl is, and at 3.30 in the morning it tasted wonderful. But with all the comings and goings with technology, it was a disturbed night; and I'd slept too much during the day anyway.

I don't have much appetite for food. I thought it was returning, but even contemplating the all too frequent arrival of the tray turns me off. I'm enjoying the fruit my visitors bring – berries, grapes and Waitrose watermelon (the other supermarkets don't come close) – but the doc insists I need to build up my cals. I've already forgotten what I've ordered for lunch, but the scrambled egg at breakfast was odourless and tasteless, and I left most of it. Now, a boiled egg, runny, wouldn't I just adore that, pity it's impractical for a hospital kitchen to cater for specific whims.

I don't miss wine, which was once such a pleasure as well as a near-addiction. Long before I was admitted here, I'd more or less forsaken it. Even then my body was telling me something I didn't want to know. I remember when and where I had my last tipple: it was in the living room of our house, cracking open a bottle of Prosecco from the village shop on my return from the Young Programme at North Queensferry, anaesthetising myself all too briefly from the knowledge that I was very, very ill and that I'd soon be in hospital or the mortuary. Three days later, the crisis broke. So my last drink was a girly Prosecco. Now I rely on Lucozade, the occasional smoothie, the richer the better, and that builder's tea, all the nicer when most builders are fast asleep in the arms of their girlfriends.

M texts. The schools are on holiday. What, again? 'But they're only just back…' – the repertoire of disbelief never changes. She's on her way here.

It looks like a beautiful day out there. My little patch of sky, of which I'm inordinately fond, keeps me posted. Dr Gillen arrives with the news that my haemoglobin level has doubled in the last 24 hours and I am able to inform him in response that I've written 3,000 words in the same 24-hour period, and so for the moment… for the moment… in overtime what one does is savour the moment… because it's all there is… for the moment, we're both pleased with me.

We talk briefly about books written in instalments, a long literary tradition commercially mastered by Dickens and maintained by the blessed Alexander McCall Smith in *The Scotsman*.

M and Stephen here. M assures me without prompting that my wish for a woodland burial will be respected. I ask Stephen how he's coping. He replies that everything is different now. He keeps his mobile phone switched on and at his bedside all night 'in case of any news'. Very sensible.

'In case of any news'… still pondering that phrase hours later. It's rather good.

Back on the machine for an hour-long iron supplement. Unless something untoward happens – and I take nothing for granted – I'll be free of wires tonight. That doesn't happen often. Return visit from Charlotte, the dietician, who finally persuades me to try one of her high-energy potions, each worth 400 cals, and I like the taste, so if I have one in the morning and another in the evening, that will go some way to satisfying Dr G's demands. As expected, can only nibble at dinner. The conventional diet is no longer working. Ask Nadia the Crabbit to bring me a full-fat yoghurt for breakfast.

6.40pm. Wakened abruptly by a pinging text. No idea how long I'd been asleep. Silence in the corridor. Discombobulating. Miss Brotherston would not have approved of such a long word, but I can't think of another to describe how I feel. Gathering sense of profound vulnerability, always associated with the onset of evening.

7.25pm. Welcome head of Alison round the door. She is off till Monday. Says I'm looking a lot brighter. I shall miss her.

7.45pm. Wonder who's on tonight. The evening ritual: staff change-over at half-seven. M texts to say she's listening to *Smooth Classics at 7*. I omitted to mention that Islay, here earlier with Fiona, says the money is pouring into the *Scottish Review*. Checks her phone: another £370 in the last few minutes. I am reduced to looking at the home page of *SR* on visiting technology. Lead piece by the excellent John Lloyd of the *FT*. Looks smashing.

8pm. This is difficult territory. When I was 13 or 14 years old, walking down a street in Bonnybridge, I can visualise the scene quite vividly even now, I became aware of a man on the opposite side, someone with whom I was vaguely familiar. I knew his name, but couldn't tell you where in the village he lived. He was a man in his middle years, nothing remarkable about him at all. We didn't exchange a greeting or acknowledge each other in any way, but I do remember that we were the only people in the street that winter afternoon. He turned a corner out of sight, and I distinctly recall uttering aloud the words: 'He will be dead soon.' And he was: without warning and within weeks. The incident so spooked me that I made a huge conscious effort to deny that it had ever happened, but it may subconsciously have influenced my mysterious decision to go to church every Sunday evening. Some months later, I had a second such experience in pretty well identical circumstances, and with the same terrifying result. I confided in no one. I thought I might be going mad. But the power of premonition of a troubled adolescent proved to be temporary. In time I forgot all about it. Until the present year, the last of my life.

In January, I'd been bothered by indigestion, as I had

been most of my adult life. 'Kenneth,' said one of my journalistic mentors, James Drawbell, 'the trouble with you is that you think with your stomach.' The January bout, coming so soon after festive over-indulgence, was so minor that I didn't take anything for it apart from the usual over-the-counter remedy: soothing Gaviscon in liquid form.

In February, I joined the rest of the Young Programme team for the annual Local Authority of the Year competition in Lancaster, which had drawn a very much higher entry than usual. We were worried about the weather – a storm was due the ferocity of which we could never have predicted – and I started to fret about the ability of competitors to get to Lancashire from all over the country. I joked bitterly to Fiona that it didn't matter what month we chose for our events, there would inevitably be a weather warning accompanying them. 'Organising events in this country,' she replied, 'is like dodging bullets.' As it happened, we were extremely fortunate. The storm in question – which was to become known as the Beast from the East and would close down almost all public transport within hours – was fortuitously delayed by a couple of days. The Young Local Authority of the Year opened and closed in benign conditions, and the standard was probably higher than it had ever been. We were delighted.

On the final evening, during dinner, I slipped away for a few minutes and returned on my own to the conference room, so recently the scene of much youthful exuberance and creativity. Last time I'd seen it, it had been a mess of screwed-up notes, discarded newspapers and left-over props. The hotel staff had now reset it for the final act: the awards ceremony. I looked down the room with the deepest satisfaction. I'd created this event. It had been the product of my imagination 13 years ago, and I was proud of having helped to sustain it through the insecurities of the financial crash and the squeeze on local government spending.

Talking to myself, I said in a low but firm voice: 'This is my last time. I won't be here next year,' and was startled to hear these words echo the full length of the deserted auditorium. I knew exactly what I was saying: not that some better offer would prevent me from attending the next Young Local Authority of the Year competition, but that by February 2019 I would be dead. I was back to Bonnybridge and that deserted street; I was again being visited – and cursed – by the power of premonition. But this time it was not the death of a stranger that I was seeing with shattering clarity. It was my own. I rejoined the dinner, where the atmosphere was raucous with anticipation, and prepared to make my adjudicator's speech. I didn't stay up late that night and felt unusually depressed in the morning. It's true that, unlike Fiona who was simply relieved when an event went well, I tended to feel down on the day of departure, the loss of adrenaline perhaps, and seldom went in for breakfast. 'After the show, the shit,' as my father put it so eloquently. But my low spirit persisted all the way back over the border; the self-revelation in the conference room had got to me.

After Lancaster, the indigestion persisted. By April I was worried, by June more acutely anxious, by July, when we went on holiday to Kirkcudbright, I was convinced I had a hiatus hernia, a stomach ulcer – or worse. In August, I consulted my GP for the first time. Blokeish, I know; I should have done it earlier, not that I believe it would have made any material difference to the diagnosis. Throughout this period, I was quietly making plans and adjustments, without telling even my closest colleagues why. I decided, for example, that the Young Local Authority of the Year, traditionally a winter event, should be moved to April 'to avoid the risk of weather disruption'. In fact, there was statistically almost as high a chance of disruption in early April. This decision created a long gap between the last event of 2018, the Young Scotland Programme in November, and the first of 2019, the Young Local Authority of the Year in April: in a busy schedule an interval of four months was unusual. Fiona and Islay expressed surprise, while going along with it. But I had it all worked out: the gap would give the team time to heal and the programme time to recover. I then set about preparing the budgets for 2019 with more care than usual, and with an eye to the long- term future, creating a more equitable arrangement for Islay's remuneration between the Institute of Contemporary Scotland and the Young Programme charities. I devoted a great deal of time to appointing a succession team of presenters for the Young Programme, pleading that I was too old to be chairing events for people two generations removed (which was true, but not my main motivation). Finally I compiled a detailed financial prospectus for M after my death, posting a file on my office laptop marked 'PERSONAL. URGENT'. By the time of my admission to hospital, I had left nothing to chance. I had already put my affairs – all of them – in order.

10.20pm. Have seen no-one for hours. Long for obs, meds, sleep. Why must they always be so late with this final ward round? It is one of my few complaints. But I have a policy of not complaining, ever, about anything. A young nurse told me earlier today that she was having a bad day. A patient had just hurled shit in her face.

The inevitable bleep of an impatient neighbour goes unanswered. Then the familiar cry: 'We'll get to you as soon as we can.'

10.40pm. 'In case of any news'. How Stephen's phrase haunts me. Shall I be gone, like so many, in the neon-lit carriageway of the night, my face covered in a white sheet to a soundtrack of anarchy and madness?

11pm. I am attended to at last. I do not care to claim that I have survived another day, for there are 60 minutes left of this one. But I'm finally horizontal, waiting for the pills to 'take effect', which I'm afraid they do with erratic consistency.

1am. Still awake, re-open the laptop. I am reconciled to a sleepless night. So what, if it comes to that? But I see that this book now exceeds 30,000 words. I wouldn't have believed it possible. Fiona asked an interesting question last night. She was curious to know if, assuming I had the time, I'd go back to the start and do the usual editing and fact-checking. I wouldn't. Couldn't. The pain of revisiting certain days, scenes, experiences would be intolerable. The thing must stand on its own, forever imperfect, dashed off like an overnight review from the Glasgow Pavilion when the final curtain hasn't quite fallen.

Friday 19 October

FINALLY NODDED OFF around 3am, revived by arrival of fresh water jug five hours later, followed by the daily visit from Eileen, the hospital phlebotomist. She asks what I'm writing, and laughs with apparent disbelief when I tell her. A cheery soul, and doesn't muck about with the needle, unlike some. Pat isn't singing for me this morning. I think she's flown to the moon once too often and would rather go to Preston on the delayed Northern service. Accept her offer of a second cuppa. She doesn't do a second cuppa for just anybody, our Pat.

Now that a target has been reached, one I'd have dismissed as impossible only a few days ago, I'm wondering if I'm due a day off this book. My fear is that if I stop, I'll never start again. The only way I finished *The Invisible Spirit* and its sequel *The Broken Journey* was by not allowing myself to be distracted by the competing demands of work. After lunch, I just shut the door of my office and got on with it. Unlike the office, there are next to no distractions in this place, so I have even fewer excuses. And I have so little time left that if I have anything to say, I'd best get on with it.

But do I have anything to say – I have to ask myself – beyond what I've said already? With normal journalism I like to get the feel of the intro right. Even if, just for the hell of it, I disagree with what I'm committing to paper, for I am a person of no fixed convictions, and no previous ones either, I'll tend to stick with a well-crafted, wrong-headed intro if it's likely to produce a piece that will amuse or provoke the reader. The idea of writing pieces to order, the conclusion agreed in advance by some committee or wholly clear even in my own head, has never appealed. I could never have been a leader writer, 'the voice of the paper'. I like playing around with words and notions too much, enjoy contradicting myself, and suspect certainty in its many unattractive guises.

This, though, the testament you're reading from Station 9, is not normal journalism. It is unvarnished wood. It attempts to tell it like it is. No artifice. No ornamentation. This has one great advantage and one obvious danger. Since much of it is straight reporting, the copy flows fast. Some of it (the observation of hospital life, the factual accounts of my own experience) more or less writes itself. But if I have nothing else to say, no profound insight to offer because I've used up such store of wisdom as I ever possessed, the copy won't come. There will be no way of busking it, no way of making it into a column, no way of facilitating a quick rejig: I'll be done.

12 noon. Jean, the palliative care nurse, is one of a posse at the door headed by Dr G. I give him a copy of *The Invisible Spirit*, the Birlinn version, and he seems genuinely touched; I inscribe it 'For my favourite doctor, to whom I owe so much'. What I owe him, and he knows it, is the determination to get on with this book when I was ready to chuck it.

I'm left alone with Jean for a chat about the weekend. She wonders if I might appreciate some fresh air, suggests someone brings me a woolly jumper and I can be wheeled down to the garden in my dressing gown, and sit there for a while, the glorious invalid, the archetype John Gielgud used to do so well. Would need the Panama hat to complete the picture. Maybe not such a bad idea if I don't look too disgusting for public consumption. Jean assures me that I wouldn't frighten the children. I have no way of knowing. I don't look at myself any more. I have learned how to shave without using a mirror if Steven isn't here to do it for me.

12.30pm. Alone again. Decided not to have a day off the book, well not exactly, but to doodle between visitors, who are due to start arriving. To this volume of confessions I'm about to add another. I've never liked the novel and have read very few and it's too late to start now; oh, and I don't feel I have missed much. My friend Jack McLean, born the year before me, whose dissolute life should have sent him packing years ago (which he fully expected, yet he is now about to outlive me) said once that he didn't read novels either. That made me feel a lot better. Until then, I'd been the original literary bluffer, talking knowledgeably about great works that had detained me no longer than the foreword. Jack's reasoning made a certain sense: what need of fiction when so much of interest goes on in real life? Not quite right, though; or rather not quite enough. What real life – the rich raw material of the streets and pubs and dimly lit upper windows – doesn't give us, and fiction does, is psychological exploration, an understanding of character and motivation, a sense of mood and place, a hint of why. In my limited experience, most novels don't do any of that very well because most novels are over-long and self-indulgent and stuffed with maddening detail. In any case there is a higher form that gives perspective and meaning to the daily horror show. It's called philosophy.

The writing I appreciate most is spare. It follows that if I have nothing better to do in the afternoon before the sports results, and reach casually for a novel, as thoughtful and intelligent a novel as I can lay my hands on, it is likely to be a slender paperback which can be consumed at a single sitting. Camus' *The Outsider,* with its modern take on the resurrection, is perfect from that point of view.

Hemingway's *A Moveable Feast*, about love and betrayal in Paris, has always attracted me for its clean prose, swift economy and underlying melancholy. George Simenon, who gets straight to the point, no messing, skilfully probes the darker recesses of the soul in his police procedural novels, without trying to impress us with his erudition. For some reason that I can't quite explain, I found James Kennaway's *The Cost of Living Like This*, about a dying man's obsession with a young swimmer, affecting on several levels; having read it I just wanted to read it again, and would have done so had the pages of the badly printed edition not fallen apart in my hands. Graham Greene's *The Human Factor*, his greatest novel though not widely acknowledged as such, had me gripped from start to finish with its heavy atmosphere of bleakness and futility in the London afternoon. It almost failed to qualify because it is longer than the others on this short list, but it is simply too good to exclude. But pride of place is reserved for *The Dead*, not a novel but a long short story. For anyone who values sublime literature, the final paragraph of *The Dead* cannot be read often enough. You learn something new about the use of language every time.

When I went to the theatre, which I once did for a living of sorts, I committed the ultimate heresy of admitting to an indifference about Shakespeare. Could only get the hang of him in patches. This should have disqualified me from the job, but there was just enough left in the repertoire to enthuse over – including Chekhov for the long farewell, Ibsen for an introspective brood, Shaw for an extended editorial conference, Bridie for a decent first act (and a lousy third), Barrie for a reliable hankie job, Wilde for a hoot. I risk ridicule by acknowledging that my favourite play is Priestley's *An Inspector Calls* (in the Stephen Daldry version), which is often dismissed as didactic and formulaic but will endure as a thrilling classic because it speaks so powerfully to the condition of 20th-century man. No wonder its greatest admirers are the young, who see all too clearly what we have done to ourselves – and go on doing. We don't love each other enough to deserve to survive. That is really all Priestley is saying, but he says it with artistry and feeling.

I thought I would have a lot more to say about the theatre; it was an important part of my life for so long. Somehow, though, I don't. Of the thousands of productions I must have seen, I have a strong recollection of only a few. I remember a towering Michael Gambon in *Skylight*, maybe David Hare's finest play; it had a rare quality of steely truth; Julie Christie, marvellously sexy in some Pinter; the stillness and economy of Alec Guinness in his last performance on the West End stage, a two-hander from America about a diplomatic impasse. In Scotland, I can hardly forget the revival, after 30 years of neglect, of my friend Ena Lamont Stewart's post-war masterpiece, *Men Should Weep*, which propelled her to fame and a certain amount of fortune too late for her to enjoy it; and, from the same producer, John McGrath, the brio and originality of the political satire, *The Cheviot, the Stag and the Black Black Oil*, with Bill Paterson hilariously cast as a Highland entrepreneur on the make.

8pm. Fiona and Barbara are having dinner together in Prestwick tonight. They put on a brave front when they come to see me, but inevitably the talk moves to 'the future' – the now quite imminent future without me. I was taken aback to hear Islay say the other day that she no longer uses the front door of Liberator House; she can't bear it. She slips in at the back, avoiding the memory of all those happy mornings when we came off the bus together, stood at the railings while Islay had a smoke, and gave a little wave to the two-carriage train from Stranraer as it rushed through Prestwick International. Minutes later, upstairs to the first brew of the morning, Classic FM for background company, and a chat about the day ahead. We used to talk, the three of us, Fiona especially, about the 'ordinary day', and how we cherished it and would never take it for granted. I don't think we ever did, which is just as well because it's over now and will never be recaptured, at least not in the same way with the same people. How lucky we were while it lasted.

Barbara believes strongly that the charities should move away from Prestwick Airport. The burden of memory will be too heavy. It will be emotionally impossible. There seems to be a general agreement about this. It is more than confirmed when Fiona announces that, last night, she found herself saying aloud that I had been away from work too long, that it was time I was back at the office.

9.40pm. The waiting hour. Indigestion bad. Linda brought me a lavender balm, which I'm applying to my wrists and temple, and from Barbara I have a pillow mist called 'Sleep Better'. Do hope it lives up to its name, which my 'anti-anxiety' remedy has failed to do. At least I'm smelling fragrant.

✳

Saturday 20 October

SLEPT BETTER, BUT TROUBLED, afraid to lie down in case I didn't wake up.

I see from my little patch of sky that it's sunny, so no doubt I shall be cajoled into an invalid outing, accompanied by such homilies as 'bit of fresh air will do you the world of good', and 'you'll feel the better for it'. But do I really want to look like death warmed up in public? As my first visitor of the day, the phlebotomist, not the same one as yesterday, reminds me, I am a well-known writer and used to be on the telly. We laugh at the implausible thought of it all and muse briefly on the Greek origin of the word 'phlebotomy'. You don't often get a discussion on Greek etymology at half past seven on a Saturday morning. If it is Saturday, and I'm not even sure of that.

Yes, Saturday. I've got that right. But I don't know what's happened to housekeeping. It's creeping on 11am and there's no sign of them. The room is a mess and this bed needs changed. Ah, here she is, the grim weekend relief. I offer her a box of Quality Street – talk about a sweetener – and she refuses it. I ask her nicely if she'll put a new middle sheet on the bed, and she ignores me. Ostensibly because she needs to get under them to clean them, she attacks the chairs with such venom that she almost knocks my laptop off its perch. She leaves the buzzer on the floor for me to pick up. She does do a mean mop, I'll say that for her. But no-one I've met in here is remotely like her. Everyone else I meet in the hospital is so unfailingly kind and obliging.

5pm. Horrible day, most horrible. In the morning, stagger on my own to the bathroom for first bowel movement since the enema and fainting fit 11 days ago. Crawl back into bed. Still feeling wretched in the afternoon and ask urgently for the commode. Another mass evacuation. Steven – what would I do without him? – cleans me up. Feel awful for my visitors because all I want to do is sleep. Am dimly aware of conversation in the room. Revive slightly just before the arrival of Connie – young nurse from Northern Ireland – who takes my BP, which is okay, and temperature, ditto. On my own for the first time today, so I'm putting down these notes – nauseating as they must be to read – to prove to myself I'm not quite out of the game yet. Window wide open admitting a nice breeze. It seems to be raining. Connie fetches iced water and watermelon. She thinks I might be on fluids by the end of the day. Can hear Steven telling somebody in the corridor that Ayr United, away from home, were beaten 2-1 by Ross County.

The idea that I might have been able to sit in the hospital grounds this afternoon now seems quite ludicrous. Am I close to death or is this just another mid-term setback? Wonder how near the finishing line I could get and still file a line or two of copy.

6.30pm. Feeling 'a little brighter', as they say, patient 'sitting up and taking notice', but unable to face food. The dietician's energy drink (400 cals) is looking at me reproachfully from the side-table; might just be able to cope with that. Barbara is on the Val Doonican chair reading a book called *The Spy and the Traitor*, while I lie here trying to summon a few thoughts about something that has been in my mind for a while.

Looking back on my life, I couldn't really be accused

of wasting time. By the age of 13 – have I told you this already? – I was Bonnybridge correspondent of the *Falkirk Mail*, being paid in postage stamps. Why stamps? Mackie, the proprietor, didn't explain and I was too awe-struck to ask. I went everywhere on foot, knocking on doors to gather copy for my column, with mixed results. The local Roman Catholic priest was always decidedly cool and kept me on the doorstep in all weathers. Others, anticipating my visit, for I was as regular as the insurance man, came to the door armed with their scribbles, and I was despatched without ceremony to decipher the domino league results or the monthly meeting of the SWRI with its 'omnibus vote of thanks'. The primary school headmaster invariably invited me in for a chat, giving my bottom a pat on the way out. But no-one seemed to need or want any of my stamps. It was a mystery.

I started work officially at 16, was working for a local evening paper at 18 and a national daily at 19. By 22 I was a press officer and a home-owner. By 24, I was a father for the first time and starting my own theatre magazine and professional theatre company. Two years later, I was a father for the second time and broke. By 27 I was presenting the news on television. By 36 I was launching a local radio station. By 38 I was out of a job and facing burnout. But I couldn't afford the luxury of burnout, and so I established a publishing business, creating the biographical reference book, *Who's Who in Scotland*. All this before the age of 40, with much more to come: the *Scottish Review*, the Institute of Contemporary Scotland, the Young Programme.

I pause here to reflect. Why did I feel the need for this whirlwind of activity? Who in their right mind would take on so much from so young an age without any apparent career path or coherent objective? James Drawbell began his book, *Scotland Bitter Sweet*, with a character study of this strange young man – me – using as its starting point a meeting between us in Edinburgh, in the tea lounge of the North British Hotel (as it then was), in the early weeks of 1969, at which I unfolded my plans for the theatre magazine. Jimmy became a keen supporter of the project, attending our little launch party in the living room of our semi-detached in Inverkeithing, where the cabaret was provided by Diana Ross, though not in person. Jimmy's portrait of me in the book was generally flattering, though he thought I should get something done about my bad teeth. He claimed to see in me a modern equivalent of the Scottish lad o' pairts, anxious to get on in the world and make a name for himself. He liked the idea of a young Scotsman in a hurry. Later he went cool on me when I joined the BBC: too establishment perhaps, not what he had hoped for me, and we saw less of each other.

There was a flaw in the lad o' pairts theory. The lad o' pairts didn't stick around in Scotland; like Drawbell himself, he took the high road to London, where the opportunities were greater, the money bigger, the girls prettier, the streets more colourful, the night life more enticing, the whole scene more alluring and with the great virtue of anonymity and freedom. I saw a succession of my colleagues get up and go, including the brightest of the lot, Ian Jack. I also noticed over the years that precious few ever returned. I felt sad and increasingly isolated, yet I was never tempted to take the same high road myself, even when I was given the chance.

What kind of lad o' pairts was this? What was wrong with me?

I cannot claim ever to have felt patriotically Scottish. When my mother took me to the Co-op and peremptorily invited me to choose between trousers and a kilt, and I chose trousers, I may have been making an early political statement without knowing it. The notion that I should feel 'proud' to be Scottish, as so many did, seemed the height of absurdity when being Scottish was simply an accident of birth. That wasn't to say that I couldn't or shouldn't support the idea of home rule, if it was clear to me that the place where I happened to have been born would be better governed independent of the somewhat larger accident of birth called England. Nor did it mean that I couldn't play a part in the public life of my accident of birth. I did that too. But the flag-waving and the xenophobia and the 'Wha's like us' mentality, among the many other unpleasant side-effects of being 'proud' to be Scottish, repelled me.

So I didn't stay in Scotland because I was emotionally committed to the country and could never leave it. There must have been another reason for my want of adventure, my failure to live up to James Drawbell's high expectations.

Was I just an incurable provincial? It's true that, in all of my 73 years, I lived in a city only once and only briefly, and you might argue that Portobello (a coastal suburb of Edinburgh) hardly counted. I was brought up in a village and went on to live in a succession of other villages or small towns, and always found the life of such places more to my taste. I preferred their intimacy and familiarity to the anonymity and speed of urban life. Ian Jack, in his *Guardian* piece, noted perceptively that I had chosen a low-profile existence, running my various enterprises from modest offices in obscure places. How well he knows me.

So that must be it: a prosaic answer to a fairly interesting question. But now I am looking over my notes for the last few hours, and see that I haven't answered the question I posed in the first place. The original question was why I charged at life at so ridiculously full a tilt from so early an age. It wasn't, as it seems to have been for many young people, a presentiment of early death and a compulsion to pack in as much as possible while there was still time; in any case, most intelligent young people would not have been so daft as to bury themselves in work, work and more work, as I did. They would have sought pleasure, travel and study as well as work: a balance.

What on earth made me so driven a personality? Here I must revisit my Bonnybridge childhood. Was I simply obeying my father's injunction, drilled deep into my sub-conscious, to 'Be Somebody'? I was never sure which somebody he wanted me to be – I never got around to asking him – so I may have drifted from one somebody to another in the hope that one day the right somebody would turn up. And now, here at the end, I have no idea whether any of the somebodies gave him any sense of pride or satisfaction in his son: whatever I did, he never had a great deal to say about it. Perhaps my real somebody – the one that would have made sense of everything – was destined to remain elusive.

10.20pm. Checklist: buzzer, mobile phone, pee bottle, sick bag, tissues, spare pyjamas at the ready in case of emergency. Have I forgotten anything? My feet are sticking out of the bed. How white they look. And now, dammit, I can't find the eyemask to block out the emergency lighting.

✳

Sunday 21 October

HOW DISPIRITING to be wakened by the domestic from Hell, bearing a water jug. She'd be better employed in a prison. I won't trouble you with my experience on the commode this morning. Overcome by the usual exhaustion. Sleep on and off for most of the rest of the day. Can't help myself. M visits with Stephen and Christopher in the afternoon. It is hard for S and C to find anything new to say. Within minutes, they are off to the cafe. I don't blame them.

This is the first time since I started keeping this diary that I feel I don't have the will to do it. Evening will be the test. I write most of this stuff then, once my visitors have gone and Station 9 is quiet.

Well, evening is here and I'm not writing.

Monday 22 October

LAST NIGHT HELLISH in every department. Hazel tells me later that I briefly passed out over the commode. Agree that we don't use it any more. Bedpan from now on, my needs supervised by Audrey and Nadia.

Mid-morning visit from Dr Gillen, who remarks on my grey pallor and general evidence of decline since he last saw me on Friday. He proposes to order two units of blood and to prescribe two new pills, one to improve my blood pressure, the other to stimulate my (very poor) appetite. He also hints at a visit to endoscopy for further treatment. But the mood of the meeting is subdued. We both sense the law of diminishing returns without admitting it to each other. One day soon, the good doc will run out of options.

After the first of the transfusions, I feel revived enough to type up these brief notes.

Islay lets me know what's in this week's edition of the *Scottish Review*. I affect an interest.

Tuesday 23 October

LAST NIGHT SAT BOLT UPRIGHT most of the night, afraid to move, listening to the terrible suffering of my neighbour across the hall. He treats the poor nurses very badly, shouting and swearing at them. I can hear Stornoway Christina, sweet Christina, doing her best for him and getting dog's abuse in return. Earlier in the evening, she and I had a chat in my room and exchanged sad, knowing smiles. She had little to say about her visit to the champagne bar.

This morning, feel quite desperate and am frank with Alison, the nurse I probably confide in most. 'I've had enough of this,' I begin. 'What's the point of going on?'

'Stay for us, Kenneth,' she says, smiling encouragement. 'It's always worse in the morning, especially if you've been deprived of sleep.'

Unexpected visit from a junior doctor, one of this hospital's production line of tall, handsome young medics. This one never smiles and finds it necessary to inform me that my tumour is inoperable, a fact of which I was made aware weeks ago. He seems anxious to impress me with his knowledge of the case and its hopeless prognosis. The insensitivity upsets me. I can't wait for him to go.

I tell Alison I wouldn't mind a talk with Doc Gillen if he could spare a few minutes. Hazel is with him. I repeat that I am on the point of defeat and ask for some advice on how my exit from this world can be 'facilitated'. Of course it is the wrong word. The NHS doesn't 'facilitate' death, but he assures me that it is skilled at making the patient as comfortable as possible. He gives me a brief lowdown of my clinical condition: it remains fairly stable (while adding that it could change abruptly) and there is no need at the moment for a return visit to endoscopy. Then an interesting question: is there anything that still metaphorically gets me out of bed in the morning? My writing?

I reply I've more or less given up on my writing, that I no longer have the energy. Don't give up, he seems to be saying. Keep going.

'I'm now nauseated by food,' I remind him.

'Yes,' he agrees, 'that is an issue,' reminding me that I had started to receive a pill to deal with the problem. I consume so many pills and potions I have given up trying to understand what any of them are for.

Then he says: 'Why don't you try a dry sherry in the evening? That might whet your appetite.'

One of the doc's little jests?

'Not at all.'

Well, that does cheer me up.

'Don't over-think,' counsels Hazel.

Doze for most of the afternoon, with my eyemask on, until the arrival of a sergeant major type declaring that my room is a disgrace, in a worse state than her teenage son's, and that she proposes to change my sheets at once. Which she and her assistant proceed to do, rolling me from one side of the bed to the next, quite unceremoniously, until the job is accomplished. Feel altogether better for this salutary experience of tough love, even if the sense of wellbeing is temporary. After their departure I note that my clothes have been packed away in a cupboard and my dressing gown is no longer draped over the Val Doonican chair but neatly hanging up.

Fiona's mum is unwell, but Fiona still finds time to call in after work. I tell her how much this means to me – and how much she means to me. She looks extremely tired, worn out.

I want to go. I don't want to go. I want to go. I don't want to go. I want to go. I don't want to go, I want to go.

Wednesday 24 October

LAST NIGHT THEY GAVE ME the sleeping draught in sinister black liquid form, and it worked a treat. Into delicious oblivion pretty well immediately and then six hours of unbroken sleep. Woke up around 5am imagining either that I'd been watching the film, *The Best Exotic Marigold Hotel*, or that I was actually appearing in it. Weird sensation. Throat parched and I beeped for hot sweet tea, which I appreciated as always. Snoozed until the arrival of Audrey about 7.45am with much snapping on of fluorescent lights, brisk opening of doors and hearty exchange of greetings. Another day in paradise begins with usual incantations of

'Good morning, ladies' – a women's ward seems to be nearby although I've never really worked out the geography of this corridor.

Overhear someone say that the clocks go back this weekend. Soon it will be officially winter. Have lost all sense of the momentum of time and season. 'Where has the year gone?', asks the cleaner. I know where mine went – in a blur of increasing anxiety and panic. And I know where the rest of it is going too, what little is left of it.

A new experience this morning: a bed bath. The Sergeant Major (Karen) and the indomitable Audrey enter my room in full parade ground mode, pull the curtains tight shut, and announce that I am to be scrubbed from head to toe, nothing left unexamined or to chance. I do exactly as I'm told, just lie back and turn over to order, listening to a running commentary on the strange case of the constipated cow. Poor cow. I know how she must have felt. Once I've been done, I am given clean sheets and fresh pyjamas. A few weeks ago at this hour on a Wednesday, I was supervising the production of the *Scottish Review*, a person of some influence in the land. Look at me now. Naked and helpless only a few miles from what used to be my office. In a strange way it amuses me, this total surrender. And how easily one adjusts to it – even to the indignity of excreting into a bedpan because one can no longer cope with getting out of bed and onto a commode.

'Enjoy your bath?' asks Alison, smiling broadly.

'It was something to have done to me,' I reply, with a slight adaptation from Dr Johnson. Spend next hour in recovery mode before the arrival of Linda and David, then Islay with news of the *Scottish Review* and Fiona, looking less tired. Fiona reveals that there are two Scott McFarlanes in the delegate group for next month's Young Scotland Programme at Troon (to say nothing of three Nicoles). It would have been my 100th Young Programme event, and my swan song. But I no longer regret that I shall not be there and am reconciled to the possibility that I won't even be alive to hear about it. What so recently obsessed and delighted me in its every detail – my pride and joy – is somebody else's baby now. It is the only way to deal with it: to let it go.

Neither Islay nor Fiona has been in my office all week. They can't face it unless to withdraw a file from the storeroom. It was once such a happy, productive place, of jolly impromptu lunches and inspirational talk about the future. Now it is kept locked and my colleagues stick to their own quarters for mutual comfort.

I can't think about this without feeling sad, so I think instead of the remark of one of the nurses. 'Kenneth, you are peeing for Scotland,' she observes. 'Then it is my only representative honour,' I respond, 'even if it has come comparatively late in life.'

Ponder my un-blokeish lack of interest in the acquisition of possessions. When my wife of 51 years, Margaret, comes to clear out my belongings, she won't find much. One visit to Oxfam might do it. I think in the whole of my life I bought one suit, a cheap one at that. I took a certain pride in the style known as smart casual – some not bad-looking jackets over the years – and the *Sunday Post* once complimented me on my ties, the ones I wore on television, but I could never be accused of lashing out on clothes. Nor did I ever own a car or learn to drive; I did half-heartedly acquire a provisional licence but did nothing with it. I might have enjoyed messing about in boats – I once eyed a clapped-out fishing vessel in Girvan harbour and thought what fun it would be to own it and paint it and constantly tend it as long as I didn't have to take it anywhere. I would have adored sleeping in it, with only rough blankets for cover, tossed by the waves, comforted by the harbour lights, with a nice fry-up for breakfast. I considered making enquiries about buying it, but didn't. It was the nearest I ever came to male eccentricity. Gadgets of the kind that absorb and fascinate other men bored me, and I never learned the rudiments of plumbing and wiring and the other practical tasks that help to justify the male existence. The only objects that delighted me were books, none more keenly than a book fresh from the press, its shape and cut and feel and the first turn of its pages and especially its smell, and if the book happened to have been published or written by me, the aesthetic satisfaction was complete.

Hope to return to this theme of extreme apathy about possessions, but meanwhile I must face the ordeal of dinner. Manage to get through half a bowl, quite a deep bowl I convince myself, of lentil soup and nibble away at a lemon meringue pie, enjoying neither, taking regular swigs of tea and Lucozade. But then a sudden inspiration: one of my favourite tastes in the world is Saint Agur cheese. I can't believe that would have deserted me. Maybe I'll ask Fiona to buy some in Sainbury's for a special treat tomorrow, preceded by the Doc's recommended tipple. Still contemplating this prospect when Hazel appears with a sherry glass from her house for my use. It belonged to her granny. Such a simple, thoughtful gesture – I shall treasure it.

I have written 1,000 words today so far. I am not gathering strength – far from it, I'm afraid – but I seem to be gathering speed a little after a rotten few days.

The running total is 36,000. Dare I hope to make 40,000 before I'm finished? I want the book to be dedicated to the magnificent team on Station 9 at Ayr Hospital – my friends at the end. Audrey comes in to say goodnight, followed by Alison – the usual stab of insecurity when one of my favourites says she won't be around for a few days – and then Hazel, who introduces me to her son Jack, a tall, good-looking boy, well-spoken, a student at Kilmarnock College, who plays junior football for Annbank and has ambitions to join the police. I tell Jack with the utmost sincerity that he has a wonderful mother.

8pm. Returning to this theme of possessions and my lack of interest in them. You know already that I don't have the time or inclination to go back and sub this book, and I've already forgotten a lot of what's in it, so forgive me if I've said this before: but I always had an unusually strong sense that my tenure on this earth was temporary and that I should live my life accordingly, without accumulation of unnecessary baggage. A gentle man called Jim Caris, a delegate on the Young Programme years ago, delivered a touching speech on the death of a friend. He said the experience had made him realise what we were all doing here. We were in Jim's words, just 'passing through'. The speech ended with these words, reducing us to silence. I thought then, had thought before, think still, that if all we were doing was passing through, best to do so lightly and with few concessions to materialism. It was a silly bloody way to conduct a Western civilised life, I realise that, tentative, unadventurous, even a bit feeble, there was at the centre of it a reluctance to embrace joy, but it was the only way I knew and there is no point in regretting it now.

Maybe something else influenced my Spartan outlook. I was never impressed by the outward trappings of people in power, how they exhibited their position through the donning of extravagant robes. This looked ridiculous in parliament and academia, but in the judiciary it was actually harmful, setting these fallible characters above the common run of men. As a young journalist I saw them daily strut the benches of the High Court in Glasgow, grim-faced, self-satisfied with their lofty position in society, sporting the ostentatious crimson of the Scottish judiciary, often flawed if not downright perverse in their reasoning and imposing sentences that left little if any hope of rehabilitation. At a lawyers' dinner we were both addressing, I observed one of them close up, a judge in the Court of Session, and thought him vulgar and cynical, with the bray of a pig. The act of sentencing, which seemed to arouse an orgasmic excitement in many of my colleagues, repelled me. The press benches were just behind the dock, so the journalists had a perfect view of the opening of a trapdoor down which the convicted man was crudely bundled, often to the accompaniment of primal screams from the public benches. Sometimes he would turn defiantly to wave. Within an hour or so, on arrival in Barlinnie prison, he would be strip-searched and placed in a holding cell scarcely bigger than a dog kennel, before being marched with other arrivals along a long corridor to the next stage in the degrading process, the introduction to such rituals as slopping out. Back in court, the judge in his chambers would be sipping a consoling sherry, content that justice, however distasteful, had been done. But always, when I tried to imagine these two extremes of humanity, I could see little difference. Under the prison garb, there was often the product of a wretched environment, a disgraceful education system, extreme social and economic disadvantage. Under the robes, there was often an unprepossessing little man in his underpants: privately educated, of no discernible intellectual merit, pompous, conventionally learned, but not often conspicuously wise.

11pm. The obs and meds are so late tonight that I'd rather forgotten about them. Haven't seen anyone in hours. But I am too weary to go on writing, and it's been an emotional day, so I lie and wait with all the familiar fears racing around my exhausted brain.

Thursday 25 October

LAST NIGHT'S SLEEPING POTION came in a dark green phial whose contents were squirted into my mouth. Got to sleep at once, but the effect not as long-lasting: woke around 2am convinced that 'Lazarade', the trendy new brand of Lucozade, is a deadly toxin and must be exposed. Once I had decided that I was not being poisoned, struggled to return to a comfortable position. Pat says mine is one of the oldest beds in the hospital – it has been in use since the place opened in the mid-1990s. Did no more than nap for the rest of the night but felt fairly rested first thing – it helped that my noisy neighbour across the corridor was silent for a change – and enjoyed a full-fat yoghurt and watermelon for breakfast, so perhaps appetite making a partial return. Fiona rings to say she will pick up the Saint Agur for this evening's wine and cheese party.

Shaved. Steven seems to have disappeared from my life, but has left several canisters of foam – in fact I'm drowning in Steven's foam, as others are smothered by his pillows – and I manage well enough on my own.

The young medic from Unst, Dr Scott I think her name is, wearing a very pretty dress this morning, checks heart and lung function, asks if I'm feeling any pain (no, except in the upper thigh of the leg with the varicose veins), and prods at my stomach. I invite her to join me for an early evening sherry in room 310, assuring her that it is medically approved. She smiles. Expresses some interest in the book, wonders where I am with it, how much I have left to do. 'Flexible,' I reply. 'It's written in diary format, so if I peg out suddenly, the last entry is where it stops. Though I'd rather it had a proper ending, a summing-up if I can think of any.' She seems to take this impromptu editorial approach in her stride.

Audrey's my next visitor, offering to order a new bouncy mattress in case my bum develops bed sores; apparently it's already a bit red. I accept. As far as I'm concerned, Audrey's word is gospel. She already knows more about my rear end than any woman has a right to know.

The dietician calls to inquire about my food intake. 'Awful,' I admit, 'but I'm determined to take your supplement this lunchtime because I know it's worth 400 cals.' Which I duly do. Not exactly enjoyable, but I manage it which I wouldn't have done yesterday. Washing it down with Lucozade makes it more palatable, but indigestion afterwards. Immediate relief with a pill and a shot of Gaviscon.

You see how the morning goes in here. Not much rest for the wicked or the dying. Every few minutes, the door swings open with another enquiry after my welfare. Maybe just as well: when I settled down for a snooze, I came to after maybe quarter of an hour with a feeling of the deepest gloom and pointlessness. Utter blackness. The terminally ill need to be constantly distracted or, in my case, distract themselves.

A question has been puzzling me throughout this chronicle, but I haven't felt like facing it until now. Why was I never able to write a successful play? It was a serious ambition when I was young and I had no doubt that it was part of my destiny – grand word. Some of the material I wrote for *Scottish Theatre* magazine I presented in the form of imaginary satirical exchanges (there was always plenty to be satirical about in Scotland), and James Drawbell told me that it showed real flair, that I was a natural writer of dialogue. Year after year, I promised myself that I would drop everything and write that play, and year after year I never did. The problem was simple but I found it difficult to acknowledge: I had no natural gift for fiction. The knack for speakable dialogue was there, but without characterisation and plot it meant nothing.

One night in a hotel, with no inclination to go out on the town and reduced to staring at an empty screen, I typed the words 'The Coast Road', and began to write a play about a young, able Labour MP, a woman tipped for great things, who made a fatal error of judgement on her way back from a meeting, killed a man on the road, failed to stop after the accident, and then attempted, successfully, to cover up what she had done. Not the most original theme, perhaps, but allowing me to explore the conflicting demands of pragmatism and idealism and how ambition is ultimately a killer, literally and metaphorically in this case.

I was reasonably satisfied with the finished work and sent it off to a couple of dozen companies, including the National Theatre and the Royal Court. There were outright rejections (neither of those institutions thought much of it), but also encouraging and fairly detailed critiques from others, pointing out what was wrong with the script and how it could be put right. Richard Eyre, who I knew slightly from his early work at the Lyceum in Edinburgh, kindly agreed to read the play and suggested that there was something there, and that the obvious stage for it was Hampstead, so off it went to Hampstead, and back it came a few days later. But there was definite interest on the part of the Soho Theatre, whose director made constructive proposals and hinted strongly that, if the obvious flaws could be remedied, she would consider it for production. I was stupid about it. I decided that I didn't have time to rewrite *The Coast Road* for the nice people at the Soho Theatre and ever after it gathered dust in my office, one of the missed opportunities of my professional life. I have never looked at the script since.

A much more promising opportunity arose a few years later when it occurred to me that my book, *The Invisible Spirit*, on the life of post-war Scotland, could be adapted for the stage, perhaps as a solo work for a virtuoso performer. The actor I had in mind was Bill Paterson. I dashed off a first draft and sent it to him. Next time he was in Glasgow, we met in his hotel and he said he would like to be in the play but that he wasn't up for a one-man show, that he would prefer a three-hander. He suggested that his friends Siobhan Redmond and Alex Norton would be interested. To me, this was a dream team. Within days I'd reworked the play with these actors in mind. Bill wasted no time in arranging a reading at his home in north London. It went well and the four of us celebrated over lunch at one of Bill's favourite restaurants in Highgate. Siobhan announced that it was a 'no-brainer' – this was an obvious initiative for the National Theatre of Scotland (NTS). Alex went further, declaring that only NTS could do justice to the script. We sent a joint approach offering our services and received a formal acknowledgement, not from the NTS director but from one of his deputies. We heard nothing more for weeks; it was as if *The Invisible Spirit* had lived up to its title and dematerialised. The weeks turned to months, and then Siobhan bumped into the deputy who was allegedly handling the project and he was positively gushing. 'Great script,' he assured her. 'We're definitely interested.' Soon after, he left NTS to join the Abbey Theatre in Dublin and the project entered another prolonged limbo.

The initial enthusiasm of the dream team could not be indefinitely sustained and I heard from Bill, Siobhan and Alex less often. I guess they must have felt disillusioned – and maybe more than a little hurt – that their stellar names and reputations were being so casually treated by a company set up, and handsomely bankrolled, to promote the best of Scottish theatre. I didn't have anything to lose, so I finally wrote an editorial for the *Scottish Review* explaining and deploring the situation. I got a letter back from the NTS director right away giving a firm undertaking that if I sent the script personally to him – the implication being that it had been lost in the system – he would read it and get back to me. I never heard from him again. Soon he too departed for pastures new.

When Bill heard that I was dying, he sent me a heartfelt letter expressing his anger at the way I had been treated by the National Theatre of Scotland. By then I didn't feel anger, only sadness. I'd worked hard for Scotland all my life. Perhaps I was entitled to more respect from people who'd been in Scotland all of five minutes. But I wasn't surprised. The two playwrights I knew best, Joan Ure and Ena Lamont Stewart, had both been starved by the neglect of the Scottish theatre establishment. So had many, many others. Why should I, a newcomer to the game, have expected kinder consideration? All the same, it was surprising that a national company, so lavishly endowed by the state, behaved as if it had no corporate responsibility to its clients – to the extent of losing a script endorsed by such prominent names. Nothing had changed. The attitude to creative people was as cavalier as ever.

5.30pm. I could say a lot more about the wider significance of this debacle, and maybe I will later this evening, but I've been overtaken by events. At 2 o'clock, Dr Gillen – although it's now a Chris/Kenneth relationship – arrived with his admirable assistant Marion for a meeting, what turned out to be the frankest yet about my prospects. Quite fortuitously, Margaret and, for part of the time, our two sons happened to be present. Chris began with the statement that we had reached a fork in the road. The blood count had again declined sharply despite the transfusions earlier in the week; in the circumstances he was surprised to find me as chirpy as I was. We couldn't go on like this (he didn't put it quite as bluntly, but that was the import). But he had a plan: further units of blood tomorrow and over the weekend to give me the strength for a major procedure on Monday or Tuesday and to sustain my work on the book meanwhile. The procedure was complicated and not without risk, and we should both understand that there was no question of a cure, and we should further understand that there could be no continuation of the blood transfusions after it, but he was fairly confident that it would give me more time. How much he didn't say. How much I didn't ask. Not for the first time I was struck by Chris's qualities not only as an outstanding doctor but as a human being of exceptional compassion and emotional intelligence. I have never met anyone quite like him. Enabling me to finish the book has become almost as important to him as it is to me; maybe just as important. The medical profession thus devotes itself to the service of a final act of creativity – a piece of writing. I ought to feel humbled. I do.

From the sherry glass that belonged to Hazel's granny, I savour the long-anticipated Tio Pepe, and soon I'm cutting a soft delicious slice of Saint Agur. Cheryl joins me in the room before she goes off shift (she's working elsewhere in the ward at the moment) and my tears fall at her gentle words of comfort. Then Diane, who tells me that I remind her of her dad, a Yorkshire miner who died 14 years ago at the age of 56. She talks to him every night. She has talked to him about me. I ask her what it is about me that reminds her of her dad. She says she doesn't know. I just do. We hope to meet again after she's been to see her mum in Doncaster; she promises me I'll be her first visit after her return to work. But 13 days feel like a long time now. I was about to write an eternity.

Overwhelming love. Overwhelming love. Overwhelming love. I am surrounded by it, wrapped in it, and I am trying at the end of my life to learn how to deal with it and respond to it. It isn't easy. It's the most difficult thing I've ever done.

8pm. Fiona has gone for the evening. The Saint Agur is back in the ward fridge. When Fiona pointed out the nature of my treat, Audrey laughed: 'What's he like?'. The bouncy new mattress has arrived for installation tomorrow. Audrey has hidden it in my bathroom in case one of the porters lifts it. That woman leaves nothing to chance.

Intrigued by Fiona's view that Islay feels I am 'away on a project'. Tempted to reply that I am indeed away on a project: the ultimate one. Sense of unreality never quite disappears.

I was going to write something about the Scottish malaise, wasn't I, as I experienced it in a small way over the adaptation of *The Invisible Spirit* that failed to materialise. Suddenly all that seems a bit trivial. If you are facing imminent death and overwhelming love, and have absolutely no notion how to cope with either, the fact that your script, which wasn't exactly a masterpiece anyway, was mislaid by a succession of theatrical managers who were not in the job long enough to be aware of your non-masterpiece's existence, feels neither here nor there.

And I must be careful not to fall into a trap. I support the idea of bright people working in Scotland for five minutes. Richard Eyre, one of the brightest we've had, wasn't here for a great deal longer, but there are still people like me who cherish his Chekhov productions at the Lyceum in the 1970s. It isn't the five minutes that's the issue. It's what our visitors do with the five minutes, the contribution they make, the value they bring to our society, and the legacy they create. You don't create a legacy by losing scripts sent in good faith. You just look unprofessional.

Joan Ure, dear, precious Joan, who died at 59, and whose delicate work is rarely performed now, was a believer in the healthy cross-section. I'm with her there. We need to be open to all the talents, the restless ones who can only spare us five minutes, and the ones who stay with us, putting down roots, as 'Scottish' as the rest of us and with a right to be free from intolerance. It's our best hope as a small nation. Actually, our only one. But I detect a lecturing tone, and I have no desire to lecture. I was never a great one for lectures, delivering them or listening to them, and I don't have the patience for them now. Though hang about. I do have a continuing sentimental regard for what I called the 'Inveramsay Lecture', which was all about the loss of branch railway lines and youthful idealism and what happened to both of them. If there is a memorial gathering in my name, it would be good if someone read it.

10pm. I've reached another milestone: 40,000 words. It's scarcely conceivable that I've written 40,000 words in three weeks. But it's a small book compared to some I've churned out. It isn't in the same league as the two doorstopper post-war histories – although academic reviewers are fond of reminding me that they aren't histories because they are too subjective and personal. To that charge I happily plead guilty.

And a strange thought to end the day with. (Apologies, Miss Brotherston. I've just written a terrible sentence. My prose is falling apart. Death is no excuse. Standards must be maintained regardless.) Anyway, the strange thought. It will be an unfamiliar experience having this book published posthumously, even odder as I won't be aware of any of the notices as I shall be six feet under in my peaceful woodland grave at the end of the village. One of the things I'll have to get used to about death is the complete loss of control. I shall have to learn to just lie there and not get too upset about the local dogs shitting over my patch. I'm not due a gravestone as such; just a simple engraving of my name on a wall, along with the names of other people who have chosen to be buried in this way. I like the democratic and holistic principles behind it. I'm warming to the whole idea.

Long ago I decided that my tiny funeral – only eight mourners – should be conducted by Chris Batchelor, a former neighbour of ours, who happens to be a spiritualist minister. For reasons more than adequately explained earlier, I couldn't tolerate the idea of some Church of Scotland bod claiming over my graveside that I was well-known in the area as a children's entertainer. Chris has some interesting ideas – including the notion that only the slenderest gauze separates this world from the next. I'm ready to check in, as long as my next destination doesn't feel suspiciously like a Travel Lodge.

Forget that. Inexcusably flip. I get like that to assuage, if I can, the inescapable horrors of the night.

Friday 26 October

A CHANGE IN THE WEATHER. I've had the window open ever since I got here, but about 5am I feel cold for the first time and ask them to close it and give me an extra blanket (and oblige me with the usual early morning cuppa). Had slept through from 11.30pm, sometimes dimly conscious that I was taking part in a competition between two dreams in different beds. Early morning text from Barbara, who is coming over from Fife, stirs me from this hallucinatory reverie – followed by the delivery of a glass of delicious iced water from Pat, who tickles my toes on her way out to fetch her mop. Not many women have done that successfully to the patient in question, but remember Pat is a woman who has been to the moon and back, so she must have picked up a few tips. Oh, and just when I'd given up on Steven, he's back. I tell him all about the wine and cheese party in my room last night, which turned out to be a one-man party despite the invitation I issued to Audrey. She's still threatening to give me the new springier mattress today, which will first necessitate getting me out of bed. Promises to be the challenge of the morning. I'm dreading it already.

'Today I'm going to write the story of my life,' sings Pat wistfully as she cleans the room. 'And it's going to be a best-seller.' Adding: 'How I wish this shift was over.'

'What are you writing today?' she asks.

'Oh, just getting on with the book.'

'What's it about?'

'Life and death, mostly the latter.'

'Can I have an autographed copy?'

'Sadly, I won't be alive when it's published.'

'Don't say that, Kenneth,' she replies with feeling.

Rather than pursue this exchange, she retreats into the bathroom, and I can hear her humming and sighing. Count the number of pills Lisa has given me. Four including one or two teeny ones. What on earth are they all for? I don't ask. Best not. Pat returns, informing me that she lives in the hills above Patna (ex-Ayrshire mining village, despite its exotic name) with her husband, a former commercial fisherman, now unfit for work. Sometimes in winter they're cut off by snow and Pat has to embark on the first part of her early morning journey on foot before she can pick up a bus to the hospital.

See from my patch of sky and the unusual brightness of the brickwork opposite that, though colder, it's a beautiful autumn day. Maybe if there's a demand I should sign some copies of the book before I go, for nice people like Pat. Make a note to talk to Fiona about this possibility if she doesn't think it too ghoulish. But how bloody silly can I get: the book won't be ready, will it? I'm losing it, in more ways than one.

A friend who died a couple of years ago, a very devout Catholic convert this man, had a specific take on Heaven. He said that God would grant to each of us a permanent view – by means of a sort of celestial satnav as I understood it – of our favourite place, so that we might observe not only the bigger picture – the changing of the seasons and the vagaries of the weather and so on – but the tiniest detail – the momentary shadow cast by a tree, for example, or the contours and fragrance (I think we're to be allowed the sense of smell) of a flower. There would be no feature, however subtle and transient, of this scene that we would miss: all of it, in its infinite variety and interest, would be ours to access and marvel at forever. The more I thought about my friend's vision the more it appealed to me, and one supposed that there would be a facility for switching on and off, resting and returning as one pleased.

This set me wondering which scene I'd choose. A difficult call. I'm not a city man as you know, so that rules out urban Scotland. Perhaps the coast of South Ayrshire, so often serene in summer and elemental in winter, a scene intimately familiar to me, with such landmarks as Turnberry lighthouse and Ailsa Craig and Adam's majestic Culzean Castle to appreciate, and allowing me glimpses of the many delightful inlets and harbours, and the pleasure of seeing the old fishing boat at Girvan that I half thought of buying, for I'd insist on it as part of my eternity – all that felt fairly heavenly. I'd never tire of watching the movement of the tides and I'd be able to recall dawn May Day walks along the prom at Prestwick with M, the rain and bitter wind lashing our faces, the only people idiotic enough to be out in it. Yes, if I could prevail on God to arrange a wide enough vista that I could somehow take in all of this, and being greedy about it, more, for I was always thrilled by the first glimpse of the estuary from the high road above Loans on a sparkling spring morning, I'd probably settle for my adopted home, Ayrshire.

But I'd have to consider other places on my short list: the walk from the station down into Plockton; the incomparable trek across the top of Scotland from Durness to Wick, a rather wintry heaven that one; the hidden gems of Galloway, but maybe not enough there to sustain one's interest indefinitely; and for sentimental reasons, Nethy Bridge, with its memories of holidays long ago, smoke in summer from chimneys on corrugated iron roofs, bright flags fluttering on the tiny nine-hole golf course, close to good walking in wild country. And I mustn't forget England at its most enduring and seductive, the view from the dining room of the Tebay Hotel in Cumbria: I could feast on that forever.

Audrey calls about the mattress. I say frankly that I'm tired and don't feel up to the exertion of getting in and out of bed until I have the first of the blood transfusions later today. Lisa got a low BP reading when she checked earlier this morning. Audrey is sympathetic. We'll see how I feel tomorrow. I decide to put work aside. Which means that, having put work aside for 10 minutes, I decide not to put work aside at all.

I've asked Islay to order a copy of Maugham's *The Summing Up*. Not an attractive personality, Maugham, but a book packed with a lifetime's wisdom and observation, much of it influenced by his early years as a hospital doctor in London. When I first read the book years ago, I was enthralled by it, but when I looked for it in my study a few months ago it was nowhere to be seen. Odd how vacuous stocking fillers (*Private Eye Annual 1981*, could there be a more depressing title?) hang around unopened for years, occupying valuable shelf space, while cherished ones push off without so much as a by your leave. I once had two copies of Edwin Muir's *Scottish Journey*, both gone.

Barbara arrives with a fresh supply of watermelon from Waitrose, bless her, but our conversation is interrupted by some problem over the first of the three blood transfusions, can't really follow what it's about, much coming and going of junior medics, but we're still hoping for tonight. Inevitably start to feel stressed. Barbara knows how much I like Edward Thomas's poem, *Adlestrop*, which evokes a rural railway station in England in 1914, its deep peace about to be shattered by mass bloodshed, its enchanting birdsong silenced for years, all of this unarticulated but implied in the poem's few haunting lines, heavy with presentiment. She reads it so gently that I cry. It doesn't take much. We are so close to the Armistice centenary now, and she and her husband Alan intend to be at Ypres on the day.

Fiona joins us for a while. She and Barbara break some delectable cheese for me and serve it on a tissue; I nibble away contentedly, occasionally taking a sip of dry sherry, while the medics struggle to launch the long-delayed blood transfusion. In the end it is left to poor Lisa, half an hour beyond the end of a 12-hour shift, to achieve switch-on. 'Why aren't junior docs properly trained in simple procedures?' I ask as she finally goes. She is a loyal girl, merely shakes her head in silent exasperation. Her parting thought is to wish that her little daughter is still awake by the time she gets home.

Fiona and Barbara are looking forward to a takeaway pizza at Fiona's place and for a split second I wonder why I'm not joining them and then the familiar stabbing pain of knowledge. The simple pleasures. I didn't enjoy them enough when I had the chance. Banal sentiment, but there is a lot to be said for banal sentiment because it is so often true as well as banal.

I shall be wired up till after 11pm. I don't mind. I like the gentle whirr of the machine. It is comforting, and it is keeping me alive a little longer while the word count accumulates and I have a few more shores to explore. The night stretches ahead (it's just gone 8.30) and I haven't really a coherent thought in my head. The nice girl with the heavily tattooed arm delivers tea, just as she did much earlier in the day; she explains she's on a split shift but managed some sleep between stints. Night nurse Kate, who was last with me on the occasion of the great vomit, when we both thought I was a goner, takes my BP; not good, never is, but nothing to worry about. I close my eyes, but there can be no real respite. Another sip of sherry. It passes a few seconds in feigned pleasure.

David wants to record me reading excerpts from this book. At first I thought it would be practicable and encouraged him, but now I know it would be too difficult. Earlier tonight, when I read a short passage aloud to Barbara and Fiona, I was fighting tears. Yet I don't cry when I'm writing the stuff. I am as dry-eyed as I would be if I were reporting a council meeting, thinking only of the formalities of composition, even when I'm polishing off a paragraph about my own funeral. I only cry when it's done and I think it's any good – I allow myself that indulgence. Writers are only human. Some of them.

Maybe I could record something else for David – a light vignette from my distant travels in Scotland – the early morning escape from Achnasheen, say. There is a reason why, forever after, I thought fondly of that desolate outpost, where Ian Mackenzie's grandfather was the post, as Achnashite.

Extraordinary phone call from Barbara. She was in Lidl buying some mould remover – I repeat, mould remover – when a rough-looking toothless guy from White City (the local sink estate) invited her to a party. She calls him Methadone Mick; quite a nice chap it seems. You can't let them out alone for long, these girls. There was some complication over the pizza too, but it seems it finally went down a treat. For want of anything else to do, I shall be checking up on their welfare later.

Kate has just brought my meds and it's not yet 10pm. This is impressive and I tell her so. The sick don't want to be kept waiting until close to midnight before they have a chance to sleep. We want oblivion at a reasonable hour.

I think of M alone in the house. She doesn't say much about how it feels. I'm left to imagine. I try to make a mental journey through each room, but don't get very far. There are some journeys too unbearable to contemplate, and one of them turns out to be a journey through my own house. I wonder if M will stay on for a bit or sell up. Either way I can't see her leaving the village. She loves it there.

Saturday 27 October

PAT'S SOULFUL PRESENCE is missed at the weekend. The Saturday relief cleaner, never seen her before, sweeps into the room, deposits a jug of water on the side table, then sets my teeth on edge by leaving my door wide open, exposing me to a cacophony of laughter which sounds unreal – sort of canned daytime TV quality – until I realised it was coming from the women's ward. Have a thing about laughter (Bridie believed it should be kept dry: agree) and once walked out of a West End production of a play called *Jeffrey Bernard Is Unwell* about a Fleet Street lush when the audience felt obliged to greet every line uttered by Peter O'Toole as if the most hilarious witticism ever devised. Bad enough after eight in the evening, but before eight in the morning inane hilarity should be a criminal offence.

Pain first thing from varicose vein (fairly quickly relieved, though). Am then offered cornflakes – I have had my last cornflake, and I won't miss Kelloggs in the next life – when I'd asked for high-fat yoghurt. I can't face the day. I have no alternative but to face the day. I'm essentially a prisoner. I see that now. Why has it taken me so long to admit it to myself? But then the yoghurt turns up, so the prisoner is appeased.

Barbara didn't attend the party in White City after all (coward), instead having a couple of late-ish night drinks at Fiona's before going round the corner to her B&B. When she woke around 7am, the room was freezing. This latest disclosure of crap Scottish hospitality does nothing to improve my foul mood. Barbara adds a detail to the story of last night in Lidl: while she was investing in her mould remover, Fiona was really going for it, putting a fully paid-up duster through checkout.

Late morning. David and Linda here. We manage to record something after all, already forgotten what. But put too much faux emphasis into it, trying to turn it into a performance. Am-dram Roy even as the curtain falls. Fatuous.

'Are you an atheist?' I ask my sister out of the blue.

'Yes,' she replies emphatically. I knew already, but wanted to hear her say it.

'Are you an atheist?' I ask my brother-in-law.

'Yes.' Less emphatic. Prepared to talk about it; to 'use religious language'.

I'm confused. Linda further clouds issue admitting that when on holiday she likes to sit in a church and think. Why does my atheistic sis need a church in which to think? Why not seek out some delightful field of wild flowers, taking care to avoid the neighbourhood bull? Sorry, Linda. I too appreciate the solace of a church, and not long ago sat next to the tomb of Lady Anne Clifford (1590–1676), whose diaries I'd read and admired, in the flooded parish church at Appleby, reflecting that climate change had not been an issue in that grand lady's day.

'No point in asking you' – I'm looking at Barbara now. She takes funeral services for a living (bet you didn't know that), not humanist exactly, but non-religious, yet doesn't mind singing the odd hymn.

'Are you compromised?'

'Absolutely not. It's a song. I like the tunes, I don't have to believe in the words.'

'So just marginally compromised, then.'

'If you want the long answer, it's my job as a civil funeral celebrant to do whatever the family wants, and if that involves singing a hymn, I'm buggered if I'm going to tell them that I'm not going to do it.'

'Were you ever religious?'

'Yes, when I was in my early teens, my best friend was a regular Church of England attendee, and I started to go along with her. I was confirmed at the age of 15, but I packed it all in a year later. I didn't encounter what tend to be called Christian values, but what I prefer to call human values, very often in the Church of England, and I've found since coming to live in Scotland that the Church of Scotland isn't immune from the same hypocrisy.'

She gave an example: 'I was recently asked to take the service of a 61-year-old whose widower had asked the parish minister to say a prayer during the service. I had no objection to it, but when I realised we had a lot of information about this woman's life to share, I asked the minister if he could make his prayer a shorter one. His ego got in the way and he declined to read any prayer at all, so I did it.'

'Does any of that make God a bad guy?'

'No, but it makes the people who are meant to be our conduit to the Almighty rather suspect. Anyway, there is no God, so it's an immaterial question. He just ain't there.'

'So what's going to happen to you when you die?'

'I'll be cremated.'

'What about your soul?'

'I guess it'll be cremated too.'

'It's supposed to be immortal.'

'I don't believe in immortality.'

'Don't you want to live on?'

'As what? Where? Why?'

Now I feel ashamed. Pat's Saturday relief, who annoyed me so much first thing, turns out to be a gem. She's called Sandra (actually, Sarah: it's complicated) and when she comes to 'do' my room we have a chat. She's 64 and will have to wait another two years for her state pension, feels cheated by the government, works full-time in another ward and here on Station 9 to earn a bit of overtime.

I ask her if she's a believer. Absolutely. No question. Was born believing (into the Church of Scotland), has never stopped believing, can't imagine how she would have got through life without her faith. I tell her she's a nice person. She replies that I'm a nice person too.

No, I'm not. I'm too quick to judge people; always have been. Suspect Sandra only left my door open this morning because it's hospital policy to remind us that we're still alive, in my case a prompt of dubious value. We agree that I'm fortunate to have my own room and that the wards are hellish – the constant noise; the impossibility of any escape from each other's smells and habits; the grisly forced togetherness, socialism with a human bum; all day, all night – terrible, inhuman.

Anne, one of the first nurses I met in here, warm and smiley, whose husband used to run the deli in Troon, and knowing of my wine and cheese parties in room 310, introduces me to a dish of charcoal cheddar. I must admit it has the look of, how shall I put this diplomatically, an acquired taste, but it is meltingly delicious and I scoff more or less the lot, Barbara picking up no more than a morsel.

Just heard that the clocks go back tonight, another exquisite twist in the ordeal of the night. An extra hour in bed before the dawn! How wonderful!

Around 5pm, as the grounds empty around Britain, I receive a selective service of results: a text, actually it takes two texts, the second correcting a mis-spelling, informing me that Ayr United beat Partick Thistle away from home. What can I say? *Patrick* Thistle, the other team Ayr United beat today, could be a continuity announcer on STV.

Kate, on her first visit of the shift, informs me that they're scraping the ice off the car windows.

On my own now, feeling guilty that Linda and David came all the way over from Fife for 50 minutes. Kate back with the meds as early as 9.15pm, possibly a record.

I've somehow managed to get myself into a good position for both typing and sleeping, by the simple expedient of ditching most of the pillows. Tempted to call it the perfect deathbed position. Omitted to report, having so much else of importance to impart, that I received another blood transfusion, second in series of three. Then down to endoscopy again, Monday or Tuesday. Then… I think we begin to run out of thens. It's one of my favourite words, 'then' – it has so rarely let me down, always something to follow, but sense my supply of thens is about to run out.

What then?

Sunday 28 October

SIT UP LONG INTO the night writing a piece for the *Scottish Review*, a coda to my 'farewell editorial'. The niggling pain from the varicose vein seems to have developed an immunity to the meds, so might as well work than worry about the state of my upper thigh. And for the first time, not sure why, I don't have an attack of the night terrors brought on by sleeplessness. Kate is aware I'm awake unusually late, I'm to buzz if I need her, but I don't and just get on with it. The persistent coughing of a patient in the women's ward breaks the silence of the night, and the nurses are soon padding softly along the corridor. I go on tap, tap, tapping with the help of the keyboard backlight, no other source. The coughing ceases. Silence. A couple of hours pass, still writing and rewriting, until I feel overcome by drowsiness and my fingers refuse to go on typing. Look at the clock: it's 4.30am, mentally adjust the time, close down the laptop, and lapse into the most natural sleep I've had in ages, propped up on the pillows.

When I'm next conscious, the clock says 8.30am, but still old time. Not a sound in the ward. I don't appear to have moved at all. And even the varicose vein has settled down.

First thing I do is look at what I wrote through the night. Curious to see if any of it stands up. Not too bad. Best thing about it is that it clarifies various events and themes in a disjoined narrative. As I suspected it's over the top in places with too many adjectives and the pay-off tribute to the Station 9 team, though heartfelt, needlessly lachrymose. Resolve to cool the prose, just tell the story straight, and work a joke into the first paragraph if I can. A strong black tea and a high-fat yoghurt later, and I'm pretty well there. This, then, is the finished piece. Content familiar, but not a piece I ever expected to be able to write, so modestly proud of it:

It is almost a month since someone in the hospital showed me a headline in a newspaper reporting that I was dying of cancer. I knew then it must be true. I had avoided the actual word in my 'farewell editorial' because I couldn't face typing it, but there was no dodging it now. This is not a second farewell editorial – I'd rather not have the usual jokes about Frank Sinatra's touring schedule – but a coda.

When the headline crossed my radar, I was staring at a wall in a ward on the top floor of Ayr Hospital. I'd been taken there after a few days in the hospital's assessment centre, where I had received intensive care in a single room. The transfer to the ward took place in the late afternoon and was both abrupt – I got about half an hour's notice – and shocking. From holistic peace and privacy, I found myself in a maelstrom, night and day, and I couldn't cope. Many do cope. I couldn't.

My visitors tried everything, bringing me favourite films that I couldn't watch because of their painful associations, favourite music from which I derived no consolation, favourite books on which I couldn't concentrate – my hope of spending my final days reading some of the world's greatest literature came to nothing – and heavy-duty ear muffs that did little to block out the suffering around me.

None of it worked. I was sleep-deprived and desperate. But I also vowed to thank, if I still had time, Scotland's first minister for her resolute decision, against the advice of many in the medical profession, to provide single rooms for most of the patients in the new hospital in Glasgow. I now knew, from my own traumatic experience, that if Nicola Sturgeon had taken only one decision in politics – that one – her life of public service would have been justified.

When the situation from my point of view finally felt unendurable, a colleague more or less begged a senior nurse – I now know her as Hazel – to have me transferred to a side-room. I was moved almost immediately and I've been here ever since, in a room of my own at the end of a long corridor in what is called Station 9.

But what I've told you is only part of the story; I haven't come to the most remarkable part. Having rejected the films, the music and the literature, and lost all interest in current events, and without access to Wi-Fi so unable to deal with an avalanche of email, I was left with nothing to distract me from the inevitable.

I had just one thing – except in my panic I'd temporarily forgotten what it was. I had been born with an ability to write. I wondered if I might still be able to write. I opened a blank page on my laptop and wrote a sentence and found that the sentence consisted of the date. It was a start. Within a few hours it seemed I was keeping a diary. I hadn't the faintest idea where I was going with it, for this was no ordinary diary. I imagined it might make a longish magazine piece, one I'd never have to account for.

During the day, I absorbed myself in recording the minutiae of hospital life, mixed with reflections on terminal illness that I thought might be helpful to others. By the evening, when the main corridor lights had gone out and the last of the day's pills had been administered, I was still writing – but the diary had turned more deeply personal and, at the risk of sounding pompous, more philosophical. It was concerned partly with issues from the distant past that I'd never had the courage to articulate. It was also attempting, slowly and painfully, to explore my own feelings about mortality and to confront, finally confront, what I believed, if I truly believed anything.

The piece was building in length. It no longer felt like a posthumous essay for the Scottish Review. *It was beginning to feel like something more ambitious. Was I writing a book? Could I, in* extremis, *actually be writing a book? If I was, it was an odd sort of book. I had to be careful to end each day's extended diary entry with a sentence that would still look okay if the author was dead by the morning.*

My consultant, Dr Chris Gillen, expressed a growing interest in what I was up to, and as we got to know each other I found him a source of encouragement, even inspiration. He couldn't offer me a cure. His palliative options were limited. He was candid about the outlook. But I had a book to finish, and he was going to help me to finish it. An intriguing question arose: could writing help to prolong my life?

I felt physically wretched a lot of the time. I was no longer eating much and there were days when I managed no more than a couple of self-pitying paragraphs. The book was now going nowhere, stalled.

But Dr Gillen was persistent. He advised me to take a little dry sherry in the early evening, reckoning this might stimulate my appetite. It did – for the soft blue French cheese I'd always loved. My room became known as one-man party central, the sherry sipped from a glass that had belonged to Hazel's granny, the cheese nibbled from saucers or paper tissues while I went on typing against an unknown deadline. One of my nurses, Anne, introduced me to a delicacy of charcoal cheddar, which was meltingly delicious.

The book currently runs to 43,000 words, written and roughly subbed in just over three weeks. It is emotionally honest, I hope it's even funny in places, and it is publishable as it stands. It only lacks a conclusion, and I don't have one, I'm still working on it in my head. I have to be open to the possibility that I'll never get that far. I take no hour for granted.

But I do have a title. It is called 'In Case of Any News'. The easy bit – the only easy bit – is the dedication. It will acknowledge the overwhelming gratitude I feel for the people in Station 9 who have made it possible. To my consultant, to my nurses, to the unsung and the tireless who protect me, I owe nothing less.

Islay calls late morning for hug and catch-up and to deliver Maugham's *The Summing Up*. I tell her about the piece I've written and she sends it to herself via a method called bluetooth. (I don't ask.) Rather not have it in Wednesday's regular edition – she's the editor now anyway – so suggest using it as a special stand alone piece tomorrow, and she seems fine with that. Islay now in her late 30s, but retaining a youthful gloss; I seem to have known her forever though it's still only 12 years since her interview in Kilmarnock and the desk tidy tumbled onto the floor, the necessity of Islay thus confirmed in one shambolic editorial moment. Knew at once she was right; the integrity was in the eyes.

Barbara returns to Fife late morning. She will 'see me again on Friday'. The unspoken thought: will there be a Friday? How many more Fridays? Seized by fear, let her go without articulating it, but she knows. Door closes behind her, cheerful smile through the window, wave, off, see me again on Friday, or see me again never?

Family visit in the afternoon. C reminds me how much we enjoyed our trip to the Open at Turnberry in 1980-something, when a season ticket-holder, called back to London unexpectedly, randomly offered us his grandstand seats for the tournament. Remember the weather that year being particularly foul, but we did take full advantage of our good fortune. Must be hard for sons to know what to say to their dying dads. Again thank Stephen for inspiring the title of this book, and he repeats that he has no recollection of saying what he said. M confirms the failed tearoom behind the house, closed for more than two years, is definitely converting into a children's nursery, a hellish prospect that I shall be relieved to miss. Wren in the garden.

After they go, open the sherry and cheese, watch the sky darken, and wonder when the cleaners will get around to wiping the bird shit off the window of this room. 'Never,' one of the nurses claims. 'They've never reached it yet, doubt if they ever will.' Preparing to die, I have the consolation of knowing that I'll leave behind some immortal bird shit.

Monday 29 October

WRITING THESE BRIEF NOTES at 8.30pm. Unable to do anything before now. As it is, a one-finger job.

Last night, remember Lisa asking me if I was 'all right, Kenneth'. I don't know what was concerning her, but I just said 'I'm OK' and went into a deep sleep. In the morning, when I looked around the room, it no longer seemed familiar. Just a momentary thing, but disturbing. I said to Kayleigh, who had just come on duty, that I didn't feel well but that I couldn't explain how. Strong tea but nothing to eat. Had the presence of mind to text Islay and tell her not to run the piece.

Then the decision I had been dreading; to change the mattress and give me a shower. When I got out of bed supported by two sturdy nurses, I just buckled and collapsed onto a commode. They wheeled me into the shower and left me to wash while they were inflating the mattress. I just sat there petrified thinking that it was my fate to die in a shower.

The kind souls dried me somehow and got me as far as the bed railings where I bent over and whimpered. By some feat of skilled nursing, they finally manoeuvred me onto the mattress. My bowels then opened for the first time in a week or more, and after the mess had been cleared up I was given pads to wear.

I have only the dimmest recollection of the rest of the afternoon. I do remember that nice young junior doctor, Ollie, coming twice – I'm sure it was twice – jabbing me for bloods. Convinced he said at one point, 'Is the book finished?', to which I replied, 'Nearly.' During one of my more lucid moments, I found a lovely note from Hazel on my bed, and a letter from Jack McLean of all people. I also remember receiving a blood transfusion and Kayleigh telling me that Dr Gillen intended to go ahead with the procedure tomorrow. I'd feared it would be postponed.

By the evening, my mobile phone was pinging constantly. I hadn't the strength even to look at texts or listen to voicemail, so the chances of answering calls were zero. I switched off the phone for a while, but the problem just got worse when I put it back on.

In the late evening, Alison did the usual obs and discovered that I was running a temperature. 38.4. First time in her experience of looking after me. She took a urine sample and came back with the news that I appeared to have an infection. She then asked me to pee into a sterile bag. Late on I was offered a cup of tea with a reminder that, after midnight, I wouldn't be able to drink or eat anything until after the procedure.

I've had days like this before, but this one feels like a turning point.

Tuesday 30 October

4AM. FEELING HALF-HUMAN AGAIN. It's taken almost 24 hours, and how long it will last who knows. Cold. Ask for a second top sheet. Thirsty, but not much I can do about it. Lisa bounces in and suggests I get up and have a shower while they make the bed. Is she joking? I explain about yesterday. The junior doctor from Unst tests my heart and lungs, pronounces them okay, but she is unaware of the urine infection.

'How's the writing going?' she asks.

'Nice of you to take an interest.'

'Well, it's not every patient who's writing a book,' she smiles.

The book has again lost momentum because of the distressing physical distractions of the last 24 hours. I now see that I took full advantage when I was feeling relatively 'well'. But there is the shape of an ending in my mind now, if I survive long enough to write it.

Dr G appears mid-morning to confirm that I still want to go ahead with the procedure. He sounds as keen as ever. So the porters, accompanied by Lisa wheel me down to endoscopy in my own bed around 1pm and half an hour later they are giving me a strong local anaesthetic. The procedure is over in half an hour and I am taken straight back to my room and told to continue fasting until 4.50pm, although I'd already won a concession from the Doc for sips of iced water.

Audrey is at reception, gripping my hand, when the trolley goes past. And now here she is in my room, comforting, consoling, generally cheering up. That woman is an absolute star.

I don't see Dr G again today, so start to panic, but one of the juniors comes to assure me that the procedure was successfully carried out.

Christopher's birthday. His 47th. Normally we go out for dinner on such occasions. Tonight they just stayed in.

Wednesday 31 October

HAVE BEEN SLEEPING too much during the day. Wide awake by 3.30am, so I ask Heather to switch on the overhead side light to allow me to work – and she kindly provides a cup of strong tea to get me going. Dislike the new mattress, by the way. It is designed to prevent bed sores, but it requires its own generator, whose vibration can only be made tolerable by placing a pillow at the end of the bed. Does it get any more old tech?

As nothing too awful is happening at the moment – that will inevitably come later – I propose to take you back to 7 July 1776 when James Boswell produced one of the greatest scoops in the history of journalism: his death-bed interview with David Hume.

'On Sunday forenoon, being too late for church, I went to see Mr David Hume, who was returned from London and Bath, just adying. I found him alone, in a reclining posture in his drawing-room. He was lean, ghastly, and of quite an earthy appearance. He was dressed in a suit of grey cloth with white metal buttons, and a kind of scratch wig. He was quite different from the plump figure which he used to present. He had before him Dr Campbell's "Philosophy of Rhetoric". He seemed to be placid and even cheerful. He said he was just approaching to his end. I think these were his words.'

Boswell was on a mission: to achieve a last-minute conversion: 'I had a strong curiosity to be satisfied if he persisted in disbelieving a future state even when he had death before his eyes. I was persuaded from what he now said, and from his manner of saying it, that he did persist. I asked him if it was not possible that there might be a future state. He answered it was possible that a piece of coal put upon the fire would not burn; and he added that it was a most unreasonable fancy that we should exist forever. That immortality, if it were at all, must be general; that a great proportion of the human race has hardly any intellectual qualities; that a great proportion dies in infancy before being possessed of reason; yet all these must be immortal; that a porter who gets drunk by ten o'clock with gin must be immortal; that the trash of every age must be preserved; and that new universes must be created to contain such infinite numbers.'

This appeared to Boswell to be an unphilosophical objection and he reminded Hume that spirit does not take up any space. We're not told how Hume dealt with this objection. 'I asked him if the thought of annihilation never gave him any uneasiness. He said not the least, no more than the thought that he had not been.' Boswell remembers that, during a previous meeting, Hume had said to him that he did not wish to be immortal, the reason being that he was very well in his present state of being and that the chances were very much against his being as well in another state; and that he would rather not be more than be worse.

7am. Must have drifted back to sleep after typing that passage. I only remembered it at all because I was once president of the Auchinleck Boswell Society and was scratching around for a theme for the annual lecture. A few days ago, it suddenly came back to me, and I asked Islay to retrieve it from the archive.

Having attempted to grapple, sincerely but I fear mostly ineptly, in this book with theories of faith and scepticism, I know finally where I am. I am with David Hume. It is the only theory that makes any sense. Very soon now, I am heading for extinction as certainly as David Hume 242 years ago; and resigned to it. Like him, I dislike ignorant crowds, whether of body or spirit makes no difference. I'll take annihilation any time. And there's an end of it.

7.30am. A poor night. I almost feel like asking for a doctor to check my heartbeat. I'm not expecting a good report from Dr G later today, and I may just ask him for a few more days before the withdrawal of all treatment. What's the point in a continuation of the suffering? I have pretty well finished this book, so the object of the last few weeks has been fulfilled. I can go now. I think I want to go now.

9am-ish. Another foul eruption from the back passage.

Most upsetting. Steven – what would I do without him? – cleans up the mess with the usual lack of fuss and soon I am restored to respectability, but tired beyond belief as always after one of these incidents. Dr G joins me for an informal chat. Reassuring. I am not to worry, he was expecting old blood to emerge after yesterday's procedure, which he repeated had gone well. I thanked him for everything he had done and said I'd written a piece in today's *Scottish Review* in praise of the team. He came over to the bed, shook my hand, and said: 'What I have done for you, Kenneth, is a very small thing.' 'Not the way I see it,' I replied.

Late morning. When the junior doctor from Shetland came on a routine visit, I confided in her that I felt my heartbeat was quite fast. She checked it and said that it appeared to her to be a little irregular. She thought she'd order an ECG. She was as good as her word: but the young woman monitoring the results didn't seem overly concerned by them. I heard nothing more.

Evening. Perhaps the most significant phrase of earlier today is 'I think' as in 'I think I want to go'. So I'm still not convinced? What will it take after so many successive days of misery?

Try a glass of sherry, first time since the weekend, and enjoy it, but it doesn't have the desired effect, at least not to the extent as before. Manage a little cheese and half a carton of ice cream, and that's about it. As everyone is nagging me to eat, I must persevere. Though I am careful to stay hydrated.

Amuse myself – though the concept of amusement in room 310 is always to invite the next crisis – by thinking about honours. I've had more than a few. All but one of the baubles (the Oliver Brown award) I tossed in the office bin when I couldn't stand the sight of them any longer. That tended to happen fairly quickly. A couple of weeks ago, Fiona divulged that a consortium, not sure if that's the word, had prepared what she considered a strong application for a Queen's honour without knowing that I was ill. Since the process takes 18 months, I shall be long gone before the offer of any gong.

Fiona wonders if I would have accepted. Not straightforward. For services to journalism, emphatically not. You can't spend your working life pissing on the establishment then come under its capacious umbrella when you're old and complacent and have attended too many dinners with these people. For services to young people, why not? I am proud of what I created through the Young Programme, it's extraordinarily valuable, and I see no reason why it should not be formally recognised. It would have pleased my father; I would finally have 'been Somebody', officially.

But then I think of David Hume, who was meanly denied a professorship at Glasgow University because of his atheism and who left this world unadorned. If such a colossus could die happy as plain Mr Hume, I shall die happy as plain Mr Roy.

My friend Jimmy Reid, who delivered one of the greatest rectorial addresses in history, was unaccountably denied an honorary degree by Glasgow University while he was still alive. After his death, Jimmy's family approached the university authorities and suggested a posthumous award. It was politely but firmly refused on the grounds that it was not the university's policy to make such awards. Scotland can be a very small country. See Hume. See Reid. I can only say that the honour for me that counted for more than any other in my lifetime was the invitation from the Reid family to conduct Jimmy's funeral service.

10.30pm. If I negotiate the next 90 minutes, and obviously I don't take it for granted, I shall have survived October, which means that my date of death will be sometime in the bleak month of November. I'll avoid the switching on of the municipal lights, the Round Table Santa procession through the villages, and the horrors of Christmas shopping. It also means that I've endured my last 'festive season'. Truly there are consolations in death.

Thursday 1 November

NOT A CONTINUOUS SLEEP last night, but not a bad one either by the patient's modest standards. The generator for the mattress bothered me a bit at times, but otherwise a reasonable night. Wake feeling slightly yucky, and fearful of the new terror in my life: hiccups. They don't last long but they are vicious while they do, and apart from Gaviscon the nurses don't seem to have a remedy. But then I have to remind myself that I am very ill and that if the worst I'm experiencing are hiccups and a slight yuckiness, it isn't the most disastrous start to a day. Nothing is ever going to get any better, so the best I can hope for is least worst. I'm not having a lot of luck with least worst this week so far.

No morning complete without a terrible event, this morning's a bed bath, hadn't been expecting it, incredibly arduous experience, rolling over this way and that, every part of me, including the most intimate, thoroughly washed, hair done, teeth cleaning service, finally had my two-day growth shaved off, all by two young female auxiliaries, the senior addressing me as Kenny. Thought I was going to throw up, though not because I was being addressed as Kenny, asked for a glass of water midway through the ordeal. Went through this once before, but it was when I was stronger and better able to cope. Thoroughly debilitating, and no respite afterwards.

No sooner had they gone than the cleaner appeared, followed by nurse Sarah bearing eight pills for instant consumption, followed by Dr Bethany Scott, who appears to have been installed as my personal junior doc. Usual questions; usual answers. I ask if there's anything she can do for hiccups. She looks thoughtful but says she doesn't think so. We have a brief chat about religion. She was brought up in an evangelical community in Shetland, but rejected happy-clappyism; her husband calls her a teapot agnostic now; I don't attempt to investigate the contents of the pot in question. They live on the southside of Glasgow, as do so many medics who work here.

After all this activity, drifted into a snooze, quickly interrupted by an unscheduled visitor from NHS Ayrshire and Arran, Ruth, who, having read one or more of the pieces by or about me, including the publication in this week's *SR* of my hospital reflections, would like to 'learn from my experiences'. I feel like replying, 'You could do worse than read the book when it comes out, that should tell you all you need to know,' instead of which I agree to be interviewed, explaining that it can't be today because I feel shattered. She asks why and I tell her about the bed bath. Ruth looks concerned. Had I wanted a bed bath? No, I said, I would have valued a day of peace and quiet after events earlier in the week. In that case, she said, it shouldn't have happened; it was hostile to the NHS's patient-centred policy. Did I want her to have a word with Hazel? I said under no circumstances. I had very good reasons for regarding Hazel as a good friend and in any case Hazel had been off for a few days, therefore having no first-hand knowledge of how I was feeling, and besides I liked the auxiliaries, who had a dirty job to do and did it with efficiency and kindness, my only issue being the timing and absence of choice. We left it at that.

Afternoon visit from Margaret, Stephen and Christopher. The usual birthday outing to the Wheatsheaf Inn in Symington not considered appropriate; the cake for Chris's 47th was cut quietly at home. M says she has now decided to sell the house. Sounds eminently sensible. She has been in touch about the natural woodland burial, which the undertakers in Prestwick seemed to think a pretty unusual request, there being no great demand for such a wild, unkempt place. It is its wildness and unkemptness that appeals to me most, but I can see that it wouldn't appeal to the socially conventional folk of Prestwick and district, who prefer neat gravestones laid out in impeccable rows, or the clinical certainty of the furnace.

Fiona and Islay late afternoon. Congratulate Islay on the sparkling quality of the *SR* under her editorship. Fiona returns briefly after work looking very tired and troubled. Long before the seriousness of my condition was known, she had booked a two-night 60th birthday celebration in Edinburgh, including dinner at her favourite restaurant, the Witchery, with her friend Louise and Louise's daughter Robyn. She is now going for only one night and leaves for Edinburgh in the morning. She is certainly due a break. Wonderful Fiona – what would I have done without her for the last 38 memorable years – years into which we packed so much? She reminds me that when I decided to start a journal of the media heavily backed by the classified advertising then freely on tap, she speculated that we might do it after several months' methodical planning. 'No, no,' I'd replied. 'We're doing it today.'

Early evening. On my own at last. Let's hope it stays that way. Intend to cancel tomorrow's interview with the NHS woman, on what the NHS can learn from my experiences. I just don't have the energy or the will to talk. Anything I have left, which isn't much, I propose to give to the last stages of this book. Sense I won't be fit for anything by the morning.

Unhappy thought: having come down firmly in favour of annihilation as espoused by David Hume, rejecting all other theories, I remember that I'd already booked Chris Batchelor, a friend and spiritualist minister, to conduct my funeral service at the graveside. I hope he understands, I'm quite happy for him still to go ahead, but if he doesn't, it won't be my problem; I shall be beyond caring.

Late evening. Thinking about it all day: the conclusion of the matter. I now recognise that the weeks spent padding the streets of a strange city as a child unable to cope with a singular malevolence irrevocably changed the course of my life. I saw myself as invisible in the universe, a shadowy, unsubstantial figure, and when I finally returned to what passed for normality it was to a silent indifference, even hostility.

I was never the same again. I carved a successful career, or series of careers, often in high-profile roles, perhaps over-compensating for the inner darkness I felt, but they were consciously developed in areas where my skills were formally applied: as chair, interrogator, external commentator, adjudicator or, latterly with the Young Programme, facilitator. I was never easy in company, avoided parties, was slow to trust people and often rushed to judgement about them in damaging ways, and preferred a working environment in which I patiently developed close relationships with a few trusted colleagues. As Ian Jack noted, I hid in provincial obscurity and wasn't much noticed. I liked it that way. It suited my temperament.

49,000 words: I've finished 1,000 words light. Shame, but too bad. I've said all I want to say and tomorrow I will ask Chris and Hazel to withdraw the treatments and let me go naturally. I have asked Fiona to provide a postscript of my last hours.

10.15pm. Here is Kate with the meds. 'Just give me a shout if you need anything in the night, Kenneth.'

I will, Kate, I will.

EPILOGUE

I DIDN'T GET 'MONTHS'. I only got weeks. I suppose if I'd
known then what I know now, I would have been
traumatised and there would have been no book. I have
had a fulfilled life. I have done so many exciting and
rewarding things. I have very few regrets. And at the end I
am surrounded by love. I have no complaints.

AFTERWORD

AT 5AM ON FRIDAY 2 NOVEMBER the phone rang. It was Kenneth to tell me that first thing in the morning he would tell the staff that he just wanted to be made comfortable now. He had had enough. The book was finished and he wanted 'to go'.

'I have phoned Margaret and Linda.'

'What did they say?'

'They understood.'

'I understand too.'

Barbara and Islay did not hear their phones but first thing in the morning, they got the same call.

My planned trip to Edinburgh was cancelled immediately. When I got to the hospital at 10am, Linda and David were already there. We huddled over tea downstairs while Hazel had Kenneth's room rearranged. The priority now was not space for drips and blood transfusions. The bed was moved to a window and chairs were set out for the visitors that the coming days would bring. Kenneth would now be in the driving seat. No more instructions to do this or that. If Kenneth was in pain, anxious, or had indigestion, he simply had to say and he would be given whatever he needed.

His mind was made up. He seemed even thinner than the night before and was quite tense. He asked for something to calm his nerves.

We took it in turns to go in at first, each visitor mindful of giving others an opportunity for private conversation. Barbara arrived, Linda and David left in the early afternoon, I stayed well into the evening. Calmed by the medication, he seemed already halfway from us but he didn't want to be alone and the blessed Hazel arranged for a mattress for Barbara to spend the night and noted the names and phone numbers of those who were to be called when the time came. Nurses and auxiliary staff going off duty popped in and lied that they would see him on Monday, their voices usually bright and cheerful, but this evening soft and gentle.

Next morning Kenneth and Barbara had a cup of tea at 5am and he asked for his laptop – there was something he wanted to 'make better'. The day brought Islay then Margaret, Stephen and Christopher, and later, an old friend who came to say goodbye. Barbara stayed that night too but throughout Saturday he was at peace with his decision and quite calm, and actually a little brighter than the day before. Sunday saw little difference in him. He spent a lot of time with his eyes closed, seemingly asleep, a plastic cup of orange juice held tightly in his hand. Any attempt I made to remove the drink was met with resistance and at one point he managed to joke about Hogmanays when he had observed that it was possible to sleep while keeping a drink intact.

Linda arrived for the night shift. When asked if he would be okay alone in the weeknights to come, he said he would.

A little after 3am on Monday 5 November I was tossing and turning when Linda's text arrived, asking if I was awake. Things had deteriorated rapidly overnight. When I arrived at the hospital an hour or so later he had gone.

Fiona MacDonald

APPENDIX

Kenneth's Inveramsay Lecture

In the entry dated Wednesday 24 October, Kenneth describes the charity he created – The Young Programme – as his 'pride and joy'. In this speech, first delivered at an event held by the Institute of Contemporary Scotland (another charity founded by Kenneth), he explains where the idea came from and what guides its ethos.

A FEW YEARS AGO, I went on a journey to somewhere undiscovered in my own country. A train took me to the northern city of Aberdeen and another north-west to the small town of Inverurie. Even here, my journey was not quite over. Still ahead of me lay the road to nowhere, a place that no longer appeared on any map. I asked in the shops and streets for directions to this place; no-one had heard of it. Eventually, an ancient taxi driver was engaged – someone who knew the lie of the land – and we drove in silence for some miles along a straight, flat road flanked by sparsely populated countryside. And then, apparently in the middle of nowhere, he stopped the car and announced that we had reached our destination. I found myself on the platform of an abandoned rural railway station, now reduced to a tangle of weeds and broken wood.

Something remarkable once happened at this exposed and overlooked spot, and to understand what it was, I have to take you back 80 years to a very different world. In the

1920s, you could take a slow meandering train from Inveramsay to the town of Macduff, 29 and three-quarter miles distant, stopping at Wartle, Rothie Norman, Fyvie, Auchterless, Turriff, Plaidy, King Edward and Banff Bridge. If you were lucky, or unlucky, depending on your point of view, you would buy your ticket at Inveramsay from a singular young man known as the railway clerk before being waved off in the general direction of Wartle. And if you were very lucky, or very unlucky, depending on your point of view, the train would be badly delayed and the railway clerk would usher you into a roughly assembled shack known locally as Utopia.

I will describe Utopia. It consisted of two rooms. One half of it was partitioned off for sleeping. In the other half, there were two chairs, a table, a paraffin lamp, a paraffin stove, and scores of books gathered into shelves to form an informal library or study. It was, as Utopias go, rather Spartan.

While passengers waited for trains, they became subject to inquiry; and the more important or self-important they were, the more challenging that inquiry tended to be. The local minister, poor fellow, was once asked to explain the difference between the first three Gospels on the one hand and St John's Gospel on the other; what Luke meant by The Kingdom; and what proof he had that Matthew the publican and Matthew the evangelist were one and the same person. The provost of Inverurie was asked how many tons of coal Britain exported every year. A Church of Scotland missionary became involved in a long debate about India. The ideas of people like Wells and Shaw, Bertrand Russell and John Stuart Mill, were discussed, dissected and disputed. Scripture was extensively quoted and examined. All this, when all the travelling public had paid for was a cheap day return to Macduff.

Sometimes, after the last train of the day had gone, the railway clerk and his young friends would settle down in Utopia, light the lamp, and talk long into the night about everything in heaven and earth; and the only sound, apart from the sound of their intense conversation, was the occasional glug glug of the stove. One night, they discussed at length the problem about sex; I understand that, after many hours, they came to the encouraging conclusion that there is no problem about sex.

On 1 October 1951, the branch line from Inveramsay closed to passengers. They dismantled the line with the usual indecent haste. And many years after that, in 1989, a dying man called Robert Mackenzie, a teacher and radical, wrote about the shack at Inveramsay and the railway highwaymen of rural Aberdeenshire who created a library and started a debating society on the station platform. As a very young man, Mackenzie had been an occasional late night guest at the shack – an invitation to Utopia being considered an honour and privilege.

Inveramsay, then, was a curious phenomenon; and perhaps a product of its age. It was a world in slow transition from religious certainties to political idealism; a world that had just endured the unimaginable losses of the First World War; a world in which questions had to be urgently asked, and just as urgently answered. All the same, we are entitled to wonder what happened to that spirit of independent inquiry, that burrowing into everything, that outburst of thought and questioning, that longing of the young people of Aberdeenshire to make sense of their experiences, that desire for something to give direction and meaning to their lives.

Yes, we are entitled to wonder what happened, and of course, there is an obvious answer. You could say that the spirit of Inveramsay has been formalised and fostered in the great post-war scheme of higher and further education. For don't we spend most of our youth thinking and questioning? No need now for Utopia on a station platform when we have Utopia on a grand and universal scale – education as a commodity, plentiful as tap water, assessed and graded for its various degrees of purity. Yet there seems to be a problem – not about sex, but about education. The principal of a Scottish university with whom I had dinner recently admitted to a feeling of despair. It seemed to him that, despite his best efforts, and for those efforts he had gained nothing less than a knighthood, it seemed to him that, among the young – young men in particular – it is no longer cool to be bright. I thought of the railway clerk transplanted to the year 2007, a 2:2 honours graduate of the University of Inverurie, eagerly dissecting the copy of *The Sun* discarded on the platform, and discussing with the provost and minister the relative merits of this year's *Big Brother* contenders, a young man striving hard to be cool and, of course, unbright.

It is the hope, indeed the contention, of our programme that coolness and brightness are not necessarily incompatible, but that, somehow, the mass industrial approach to education needs to be softened by an alternative more intimate and more intellectually free; that, in some way, it is possible to recapture Inveramsay and reinterpret it for the modern world. All our programme seeks to do, and it is essentially a modest aspiration, is to create for a tiny group of disparate individuals, from many different backgrounds and life experiences, a climate, an atmosphere, a setting, which encourages the same sense of intellectual excitement, the same human bond, the same explosion of restless energy as was once spontaneously combusted in a lonely railway shack.

We have to believe, do we not, that some things still matter. Otherwise, what is the point of our existence? What matters about Inveramsay? What is it telling us?

Accept nothing: challenge everything: that matters.

Question authority: that matters.

Scrutinise established ways of thinking and doing: that matters.

Apply individual personal understanding to known facts: that matters.

Other more complex things matter too. The unmapped places of the world matter. The road to nowhere matters.

Branch lines matter. They have all gone as physical artefacts – grassed over and eroded by rain and gravity as completely as any Roman road or earthworks. But they can still exist in our imagination. The main line proceeds at speed to a predictable and deadly terminus. On a mainline, the light at the end of the tunnel is that of the oncoming train. Choose instead the gentle and meandering branch line of unorthodox thought and feeling. Non-conformity matters.

The cross-section matters perhaps as never before in our history. That principle which brought together the people of rural Aberdeenshire, rulers and ruled, old and young, alike. The same principle that inspires and motivates our own programme, bringing together under the same roof the jailers and the jailed, atheists and true believers, gay and straight, those who would torture and those who would not.* Bring together such a cross-section and get them talking long into the night, and discord can begin to sound unexpectedly harmonious. The cross-section – our best hope; perhaps our only one.

Inveramsay also informs us that nothing lasts. The recognition that nothing lasts also matters. The branch line to all those lovely places had a life shorter than some human spans. The shack was of flimsy construction – fragile and vulnerable – as easily destroyed as the glittering city. And the railway clerk – he was last heard of in Putney, working as a barman – what on earth happened to him? Where did all that curiosity go? All that hope? What was his name? Who remembers him now? Nothing lasts.

The ultimate award in our annual programme, the award of Young Thinker of the Year, is named in memory of a young Scottish journalist, Richard Wild, who was murdered in Baghdad. I call to mind two sentences of devastating truth and simplicity expressed by Richard Wild's father on the final night of one Young Scotland Programme: 'If you want to say something to somebody, say it now. If you want to do something, do it now.'

Of course, that matters more than anything.

* *Fiona MacDonald writes: This refers to a question often debated at programmes in the first few years of the new millennium: 'In the war on terror, is the use of torture ever justified?'*

When Kenneth first delivered the Inveramsay lecture, he never imagined that he would one day know the name of the railway clerk.

However, Barbara Millar, with the help of a genealogist friend, succeeded in discovering who he was:

R. F. Mackenzie said the unnamed railway clerk was last heard of working as a barman in Putney. He never actually had such a job. And he is no longer unknown.

The railway clerk was Allan (later changing the spelling to Alan) Gray Law, born on 7 May 1907 at Kirkton of Rayne in rural Aberdeenshire, one of 11 children. He was brought up on a farm where his father bred heavy horses. He was a contemporary of R. F. Mackenzie whose own father was stationmaster at Wartle, one stop on the line from Inveramsay.

Alan Law took up employment on the railways in 1927. His friend, the shunter, with whom he shared the two-roomed shack they called Utopia, was Bill Drummond, who was also his brother-in-law. Alan had married Bill's sister Bella and they had four children – Michael, Lizi, Alan and David. Alan resigned from the railways in 1930, left Aberdeenshire and moved to London.

For most of his life he worked on the financial and administrative sides of civil engineering projects, his work taking him to the Middle East, Africa, North and South America: he was involved in work on the docks in Port Talbot, the Suez Canal, the port in Aden and bridges in the Caribbean. In later life he and Bella moved to Winchester. He died on 27 September 1979 from prostate cancer. He was 72. He maintained a well-stocked library throughout his life. And he never told his children about Utopia.

Barbara Millar